Second Edition

Matt Abrahams

Speaking Up *without* FREAKING OUT

50 TECHNIQUES FOR CONFIDENT · CALM · COMPETENT PRESENTING

Kendall Hunt publishing company

"I learned that courage is not the absence of fear, but the triumph over it" –Nelson Mandela

To my family for their fearless support. –M.A.

CONTENTS

Contents

PREFACE

If you've ever felt nervous, doubtful, or insecure about giving presentations or speeches, this pocket book is for you. It provides you with easy-to-use techniques for managing presentation anxiety, whether your audience is composed of coworkers, prospective clients, fellow students, or family and friends.

This book was born out of frustration. For decades, psychologists, biologists, and communication researchers have documented and detailed strategies and techniques for addressing speaking anxiety. However, much of this work remains locked away in academic journals. Further, techniques that do escape to a wider audience via public speaking or business communication textbooks are often vague and insufficient. These texts present what I refer to as the "PB & J" approach to speaking anxiety management: "Practice, Breathe, and Just do it." Although these suggestions have some validity, speaking anxiety involves a complicated mix of physiological and psychological factors. Simplistic "PB & J" advice is not likely to help. Worse, it could even increase anxiety if the suggestions are attempted without immediately successful results.

I hope to remedy this lack of useful information by providing 50 tried-and-tested anxiety management techniques that you can easily put into practice. Most of the techniques detailed here are based on academic research, and all have been shown to be effective. As you read this book, you will learn several techniques that will help you feel more confident about yourself and your presentations. Your goal: Speaking up without freaking out!

HOW TO USE THIS BOOK

I applaud you for taking the first steps to becoming a more confident, calm, and competent presenter! This book will equip you with techniques that you can use to manage your speaking anxiety and enhance your confidence.

This book is divided into six chapters: Chapter 1 describes speaking anxiety, how it shows itself, its negative effects, and how you can appear less nervous. Chapter 2 describes the main theories about why people feel anxious when speaking and, importantly, offers you several specific techniques to reduce speaking anxiety and bolster your confidence. Chapter 3 explores how focusing on your audience's needs and connecting your content to them can reduce your anxiety and make your presentations more compelling. Next, Chapter 4 provides techniques and guidance on how to better remember your presentation content. Chapter 5 teaches how to resist and stop some self-defeating beliefs and behaviors that perpetuate anxiety. Finally, Chapter 6 addresses how to put all this information to work for you by creating your own anxiety management plan.

A glossary is included that will explain the more technical, scientific terms found in the book (these terms appear in *italics*), along with five appendixes. Appendix A suggests techniques for managing anxiety that comes from audiences not immediately present for your speech (e.g., conference calls, web presentations). Appendix B gives additional suggestions for those who are not native English speakers. Appendix C provides two effective techniques for reducing verbal disfluencies, such as "um's" and "uh's." Appendix D addresses how to feel confident during a question-and-answer session. Finally, Appendix E summarizes the anxiety management techniques presented (these techniques appear in **bold** throughout the book).

As you read, you will come across several *"Try this"* opportunities designed to help you put the techniques into practice. Many of the techniques ask you to reflect and then act on the suggestions made. Take your time and determine what works for you. Some of these techniques need to be used over an extended period to be effective and for you to be comfortable with them.

Last, each chapter ends with a summary of *Key Take Aways* along with an *Activity* designed to help you put chapter concepts into practice.

Please be warned that some of the techniques presented in this book seem to contradict each other. For example, one technique for reducing speaking anxiety suggests that you think optimistically about exciting events or activities after your presentation, while another one asks that you focus solely on the present moment. Ultimately, you will choose the techniques that work best for you, and you will figure out how to implement them in a way that is meaningful and helpful to you.

CHAPTER 1
Speaking Anxiety: Explanation and Manifestations

Riiiip. My anxiety level shot through the roof. It happened early one Saturday morning when I was a high school sophomore, competing in my very first speech tournament. Not only were my teammates and coach present to cheer me on, but the girl I liked was there also, to see me deliver my speech on karate. The butterflies in my stomach, the sweat on my brow, and the quiver in my legs made me more than hesitant to begin, but the prodding from my peers gave me enough motivation to begin my presentation.

Little did I know that my pre-speech jitters were nothing compared to what was to come. *Riiiip.* In front of friends, teachers, parents, and a potential girlfriend, I ripped my pants. Not a tiny tear, but a major, gaping crevasse from back belt loop to fly zipper. The front snap kick I performed during the first 10 seconds of my 10-minute speech was supposed to be action packed and engaging. Instead, it was exasperating and embarrassing. My pre-speech nervousness had me so focused on a variety of imagined embarrassing outcomes that I forgot to change into my karate pants—the ones designed to allow full leg movements.

Presenting in public, even when a speaker is prepared and practiced, can lead to dramatic and traumatic outcomes. For this reason, the *Book of Lists* has repeatedly reported that the fear of speaking in public is the most frequent answer to the question "What scares you most?" In fact, people rate speaking anxiety 10 to 20 percent higher than the fear of death, the fear of heights, the fear of spiders, and the fear of fire. As a student of mine once joked: "People would rather stand naked while on fire, overlooking a 30-story fall, covered with spiders and snakes than give a speech."

Why is fear of speaking always rated so much higher than other fears and phobias? And, more important, how can you learn to manage and reduce this ubiquitous fear?

SPEAKING ANXIETY

The word "anxiety" comes from the Latin word "angusta," which translates to "a narrowing corridor that presses down on one passing through." So, anxiety refers to the concern of not making it through something, like a presentation or meeting. The anxiety that originates from speaking in front of others is known as *communication apprehension*. This apprehension is both the real-time anxiety associated with actually speaking *and* the anxiety that comes with just thinking about speaking. Communication researchers list three distinct phases when communication apprehension is likely to strike: (1) anticipation before speaking; (2) confrontation, the first minute or so of presenting; and (3) adaptation, the last minutes of speaking. Most anxious speakers report their anxiety is highest during anticipation and confrontation and declines steadily during adaptation. This pattern of anxiety reduction is referred to as *habituation* and comes from the comfort of realizing that you have made it through the first part of your presentation without major problems.

Research in communication apprehension has shown that excessive and prolonged speaking anxiety results in a downward spiral. Beyond the negatives associated with apprehension, such as embarrassment and inability to focus, this anxiety leads to additional costly outcomes. First, not only does speaking anxiety cause you to present poorer speeches, but if you're highly anxious, you're also likely to write poorer speeches. Second, people who appear nervous are often judged as being deceptive. Many behaviors associated with nervousness—avoiding eye contact, stumbling over words, pacing around, and the like—are also linked to lying or hiding information. This means that speaking anxiety can negatively influence your credibility and your ability to make the impact you want, because people might question your trustworthiness. And, as if these problems aren't enough, being nervous reduces your ability to think clearly, to make effective decisions, and to respond to your audience's reactions.

Anxiety affects mental processing, which often leads to either panicking or choking. *Panicking* occurs when you can't seem to think clearly or maintain focus—you go blank. *Choking* is when you think too much—your thoughts become jumbled and overly self-conscious. This flustered mental processing results in anxious speakers remembering less. They remember fewer of their ideas and fewer details about those ideas. As a result, anxious speakers often struggle to think of the words and ideas that they want to express. They report a disconnect between their desired message and their delivered message.

Finally, being highly anxious about presenting affects your ability to ascertain your speaking effectiveness. Not only does your anxiety negatively skew your ability to judge your own performance accurately, but your nervousness tends to make you misinterpret others' feedback as being more negative than it was intended to be.

With all these possible costs in mind, reducing speaking anxiety is important to increasing your communication confidence and competence.

Try **Try this:** To see exactly how nervous public speaking makes you, access and complete the Personal Report of Public Speaking Anxiety scale at www.jamescmccroskey.com/measures/prpsa.htm.

BEING NERVOUS

What Does Anxiety Feel Like?

Everything you can do to reduce your anxiety will help you communicate more effectively. To figure out which anxiety reduction techniques might be best, you first need to better understand your nervousness and its effects.

What does it mean to be nervous when speaking? What happens to your body physically when you're anxious about speaking in public? Your muscles get tense. You sweat. Your heart rate speeds up. Your blood pressure increases. You find it hard to breathe. Your perception of time warps so that things seem to take much longer than they actually do. You find it hard to execute fine motor skills like using a laser pointer. These physical symptoms of speech anxiety are not healthy. In fact, prolonged anxiety such as this can lead to long-term health consequences.

In reflecting on these physical changes, you can see that your *fear response*, the physiological arousal associated with public speaking, is the same reaction that occurs when anything frightening happens to you. For example, these physical responses are the same ones you would experience if you heard your pilot say "Uh-oh" over the intercom just before the oxygen masks suddenly came down. In other words, there's no such thing as a distinct public speaking fear response. Public speaking, or your anticipation of speaking, is simply activating your innate fight, flight, fright, and freeze response.

Interestingly enough, if I walked up to you and said, "Congratulations, you just won the lottery. Here's $10 million," you'd experience the same physiological changes. Your heart rate would increase, your blood pressure would go up, you might find it hard to breathe, your muscles might get tense, you might feel butterflies in your stomach, and you might sweat. These are the same responses associated with the inborn fear response. In other words, you have only one arousal system and one way of experiencing arousal. The difference is that when you find out you won $10 million, you scream, "Yay!" When you are told you have to give a speech, you moan, "Oh, no!"

Thus, how you identify your arousal plays a role in how you experience the physical symptoms. That is, your labeling of your physiological response plays an important role in how you manage anxiety. Interestingly, researchers have found that anxious individuals tend to be more acutely aware of their bodily sensations—something they label as *interoceptive sensitivity*-and are more likely to interpret increased heart rate and sweating in a negative way.

Try   **Try this:** When you experience negative physical arousal (e.g., your heart rate increases, you begin to sweat), remind yourself that these reactions are normal and typical. This is called **relabeling**. These sensations do not show anything beyond your body's normal response to something that is displeasing. In other words, avoid giving these natural responses special significance. You can go a step further and **greet** or accept these natural responses by saying to yourself: "Here are those anxiety feelings again. Of course, I should be feeling them. I am about to give a presentation."

What Does Anxiety Look Like?

Your audience can't feel your physical reactions to anxiety, but they can observe the behaviors that result, and from these behaviors, they infer your confidence.

So, how does an audience know when a speaker is nervous? Common signs of nervousness when speaking include *disfluencies* (repeating of words, stuttering, using filler words, such as "uh," "you know," and "I mean"), lack of eye contact, fidgety arms and hands, shallow breathing, swaying and pacing, problems with speaking rate (either too fast or too slow), and plumbing reversal—what is usually wet gets dry (e.g., dry mouth) and what is dry gets wet (e.g., sweaty palms and brow). You can categorize these anxiety-produced behaviors as either agitated (involving a lot of movement, fast speech, and multiple disfluencies) or rigid (involving stilted, slow speech and lengthy pauses).

Certainly, you do not engage in these behaviors on purpose. They arise from the increased *cognitive demand* that results from your speech anxiety. You simply do not have the mental resources to cover the *leakage* of these anxiety cues. It's similar to what happens when a poker player with a potentially winning hand indicates nonverbally to the other players that she thinks she is going to win. In the case of speaking, the anxiety associated with speaking might lead you to reveal your nervousness.

How Do You Appear Less Nervous?

You can actively work on presenting in a confident manner. In acting, this technique is called "act as if." I affectionately call this approach "**fake it until you make it**." You have an intuitive sense of what behaviors a confident speaker employs. For example, you know that confident speakers connect with their audiences through sustained eye contact. Audiences see this direct, protracted eye contact as conveying higher status. Further, you know that the lack of good eye contact makes you appear nervous and deceptive. So, you can learn to fake good eye contact.

How do you fake eye contact? When at 18 inches or farther away from your audience, try looking at that spot between people's eyebrows...you know the place, where if you don't shave or pluck you would end up with a "unibrow." Amazingly, your audience believes you are looking directly at them. Similarly, you know confident speakers avoid distracting body movements. Swaying or leaning are signs of nervousness. To eliminate unneeded and distracting movement, face your feet forward directly under your shoulders, bend your knees slightly, and move one foot an inch ahead of the other. From this position, it is very hard to sway or lean.

Figure 1: Stabilizing Presentation Stance

Additionally, poised and polished speakers stand balanced and connect with their audiences through extended gestures. Nervous speakers retreat and make themselves smaller by stepping back or leaning while keeping their hands close to their body in front of their chest. Think of a boxer being pummeled by his opponent. He steps back, draws his hands in toward his body, and pulls his head down. This protected position makes sense when threatened by a sweaty, fist-launching attacker. However, this all-too-common body position is awful for a speaker. To counteract this natural tendency to retreat and protect, you need to stand upright and take one step toward your audience when you begin speaking. Approaching your audience makes you appear confident and embracing. Further, standing tall allows you to breathe fully and maximize your voice. In fact, research suggests that people who maximize the full extent of their bodies and the space around them are seen as more powerful and persuasive. Interestingly, the very act of taking up more space makes you feel more powerful. It turns out that your body releases more testosterone (a neurotransmitter that reduces anxiety) and less cortisol (a neurotransmitter that initiates the fear response) when you stand tall, lean in, and take up more space.

When gesturing, reach out and away from your body—get your elbows out, off your body. Avoid what a client of mine called the "T-Rex" position, in which your elbows are in tight next to your sides and your hands are making small gestures in front of your chest. Think of extending your arm as when you shake someone's hand. Again, extension toward your audience is seen as confident and embracing.

Figure 2: Extend Gestures Away from Your Body

If gesturing is difficult for you, start by practicing *descriptive gestures* when you present. That is, have
your gestures mimic what you are describing with your
words. For example, if you refer to your company's
growth, you can represent this growth by moving your
hand and arm up and to the right. Once you are more
comfortable gesturing, you can consider *emphatic gestures*, which add emphasis to your points. However, you
should not script emphatic gestures to correspond with
specific words or phrases. Scripted emphatic gestures
are distracting and make you appear less authentic.
One helpful way to practice gesturing is to **audio record
yourself delivering your presentation**, then play the
recording back while you stand and practice your gestures. Since you do not have to think about what to say,

practicing in this manner allows you to focus on your gestures and other nonverbal behaviors.

Interestingly, research suggests that purposeful gesturing is a great way to reduce a speaker's *cognitive load*, which allows you to focus more on what you are saying. For example, during conversations, you likely gesture naturally. This gesturing lightens your mental effort and allows you to pay attention and learn from those with whom you are speaking.

Sweating and flushing often accompany speaking anxiety as a result of increased blood flow. To address these symptoms, you can **reduce your core body temperature**. Just as you might place a cold compress on a child's feverish head or neck to reduce her temperature, you can hold something cold in the palms of your hands—a chilled bottle of water is ideal. The cold will reduce your body temperature and reduce the sweating and flushing that result from increased blood flow.

Finally, an effective way to reduce the shaking that nervousness can bring on is to **give your nervous energy a place to go**. For example, you can secretly squeeze your toes or lightly squeeze your thumb and pointer finger together in your nongesturing hand. These activities allow you to rid yourself of this excess energy and eliminate your shakiness.

By covering up or faking your way through your nervousness, you allow for a counterintuitive psychological truism to take effect: Your actions can lead to your feelings. In other words, act in a competent manner, and you will begin to feel competent and reduce your anxiety. Additionally, since your audience does not know you are faking behavior that makes you appear

competent and confident, they treat you as if you are
naturally competent and confident, which in turn fuels
your feelings of competence and confidence. Try it! Fake
it until you make it really works.

Try **Try this:** Observe carefully the behaviors of
competent and confident speakers. Note their
use of eye contact and their stance, movement,
and gestures. Practice mimicking some of these
actions and see how you feel. Over time, as you engage in
competent speaking behaviors, you will begin to feel more
confident and competent. A great source to watch authentic,
confident speakers can be found at www.ted.com.

WHAT IS BEHIND YOUR FEAR?

Academics like to create classification systems to
help explain things. Scholars have a communication
apprehension classification system that distinguishes
among four types. The first type is what is called *trait-
based communication anxiety*. Trait-based anxiety is better known as shyness or extreme introversion. Because
this type of anxiety has a strong genetic component, few
people suffer from true trait-based anxiety—roughly
only 7 percent of the U.S. population is clinically shy.
Yet, you probably know somebody who's really shy.
Clinically shy people can't take public speaking classes
or even read books about speaking. They don't have
many friends. They cower at social events. They prefer
to stay home. Thankfully, both psychological and medi-
cal interventions can help those afflicted with clinical
shyness to manage better.

For the rest of us, this classification system has three other types of *state-based communication apprehension* that are caused by or correlated with external circumstances.

In situation-based anxiety, the context in which you are speaking (i.e., room location and number of people) causes your anxiety. For example, you might be passionate about recycling, and when you talk about recycling with friends at the dinner table or a coffee shop, you're not nervous at all. But when you have to stand in front of many people and give a 5-minute speech on recycling, you're nervous. In this case, your view of the situation or context in which the communication occurs causes the anxiety.

Next is audience-based anxiety. Who you are speaking to activates this type of anxiety. Audiences vary in many aspects (e.g., status, expertise, attitudinal similarity), and some of these characteristics can provoke more anxiety than others. You might not have any trouble speaking to your peers or family members, but speaking to a manager or potential funder might cause you great trepidation. Power and status are believed to be at the root of audience-based anxiety.

The third state-based anxiety is called goal-based anxiety, and it involves what you are trying to accomplish. You might be able to talk to your boss about your work progress or even the latest football score without a problem. But when you ask your boss for a raise or time off, you become nervous. It's the goal you're trying to achieve that makes you nervous. By definition, a goal is about a future state, and it is these future concerns that instigate your anxiety.

It helps to reflect on the basis of your speaking anxiety (that caused by the situation, your audience, or your goal). Your anxiety might originate in some combination of these state-based anxieties, but one most likely predominates. By determining which one of these types is the source of most of your anxiety, you can begin to develop a targeted, proactive approach to addressing your fear.

 Try this: Think about a recent public speaking experience in which you felt anxious. Ask yourself what brought about the anxiety? Were you overly concerned with the situation, your audience, or your goal?

Key Take Aways

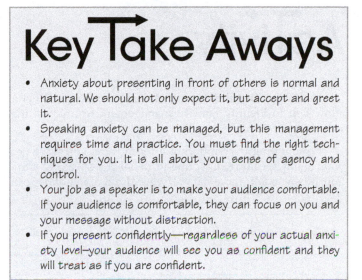

- Anxiety about presenting in front of others is normal and natural. We should not only expect it, but accept and greet it.
- Speaking anxiety can be managed, but this management requires time and practice. You must find the right techniques for you. It is all about your sense of agency and control.
- Your job as a speaker is to make your audience comfortable. If your audience is comfortable, they can focus on you and your message without distraction.
- If you present confidently—regardless of your actual anxiety level—your audience will see you as confident and they will treat as if you are confident.

AcTivity

Understanding the source of your anxiety will better allow you to identify anxiety management techniques that will work for you.

Write a brief description of a recent time you were nervous about speaking. Describe in detail the speaking situation, how you felt, and what you were afraid of might happen.

_____

_____

_____

_____

_____

_____

_____

_____

_____

_____

_____

Read through what you have just written. Circle any words that relate to the speaking situation/location, the audience, or the goals/consequences of your presentation. Count the number of circles in each category (situation, audience, or goal). The category with the most circles likely represents the source of your anxiety.

CHAPTER 2
Anxiety Sources and Solutions

WHY ARE YOU ANXIOUS AND HOW CAN YOU MANAGE IT?

Dealing with speech anxiety involves managing two components: (1) your fear of the fear, which is also known as *anxiety sensitivity*, and (2) your fear of presenting. Sometimes, the stress over being nervous is greater than the actual threat. Clearly, speaking invokes a fear response for many people. Additionally, being stressed or anxious can be frightening. So, you need to make sure that any anxiety-quelling techniques you use not only improve your speaking confidence and competence, but also enhance your ability to manage your reaction to anxiety.

Research has identified five major theories that explain why we get nervous, and each theory offers multiple therapies or ways of managing that anxiety. The goal is to find at least one strategy or technique that suits you best for managing your fear. Keep in mind that you are unlikely to completely rid yourself of speaking anxiety. In fact, you probably don't want to overcome your nervousness entirely. Your anxiety tells you what is important. If presenting well did not matter to you, you likely wouldn't get so nervous. Managed speaking anxiety can be beneficial in several ways: It helps you to focus on your speaking task, provides you with energy, motivates you to care about your communicative outcomes, and encourages you to prepare. In other words, rather than your archenemy, you want your speaking fear to be your sidekick. Of course, reaping these benefits requires you to adjust and adapt to your fear. Thus, the goal is to learn to manage your anxiety so that it does not manage you.

Theory 1: Behavioral Theory

According to behavioral theory, you're nervous because you don't have the skills or know the proper way to speak well, so you are afraid. Think of it this way: If you were a novice skier and someone put you at the top of a double black diamond ski slope, you would be afraid . . . very afraid. But, if over time you took lessons, practiced, and worked on it, you would be more comfortable. So, according to behavioral theory, the way to manage your speaking anxiety is to **develop your speaking skills**. Just by reading this text, you've already begun this skills-fortifying journey.

An added benefit of seeking out presentation skills is that you will find others who share your concerns and desire to improve. One clear way to improve your confidence and reduce anxiety is to **collaborate with others** striving toward the same goal. This collaborative approach is one of the main reasons support groups are so helpful.

Try **Try this:** Take steps to develop your presentation skills. Read books, attend public speaking classes, join speaking organizations (e.g., Toastmasters), and analyze successful speakers. By actively learning about speaking and developing skills, you will become both more comfortable with and more competent at speaking. You may wish to join the Facebook community for this book to find other like-minded individuals and learn new tips: www.facebook.com/SpeakingUpwithoutFreakingOut or www.NoFreakingSpeaking.com.

One fun and very useful type of collaboration that can help reduce speaking anxiety is to **participate in an improvisation class**. Improv is an approach to acting that invites spontaneity and active listening. Improv activities or games ask you to be silly and calmly experiment with many possibilities while being in front of an audience. Fundamental improv rules like "always say 'yes'" and "if you're going to fail, fail big" teach nervous speakers that being in front of others can be a less threatening and potentially positive experience.

Taking time to **breathe slowly and deeply** is another very practical behavioral therapy that can be practiced easily. "Belly breathing"—filling your lower abdomen by inhaling slowly through your nose—not only can slow your nervous symptoms (e.g., lowered heart rate), but by focusing attention on the inhalation and exhalation, it dampens the mental noise that anxiety causes.

Try **Try this:** Place one hand on your upper chest and the other on your abdomen. Take a slow, deep inhalation through your nose and fill your lower abdomen. Feel your lower hand expand with your abdomen while keeping your upper hand flat. Slowly release your breath through your nose and feel your abdomen contract. To occupy your mind, slowly count to three as you inhale and then again as you exhale. Focus your attention on the counting. Repeat this type of breathing several times.

Just as proper breathing can help you feel more relaxed and less nervous, **dressing appropriately and comfortably allows you to feel more confident**. While styles and fashion change, a few appearance guidelines remain constant. First, dress in clothes that conform to the requirements of your speaking situation and meet the expectations of your audience. In Silicon Valley software firms, which pride themselves on being super casual in their dress, engineers often do not trust anyone who shows up to present wearing a suit. Likewise, New York investment bankers are likely to disregard speakers who dress in cut-off jeans and flip-flops. You may need to do some reconnaissance in order to determine the appropriate attire. When in doubt, dress more formally. Second, remove distracting items, such as watches, jewelry, and pens. Nervous speakers often fiddle and futz with clothing accessories. Along these lines, if you have long hair, please consider pulling it back.

Speakers who constantly brush or blow their hair out of their faces appear distracted and less confident. Next, find a pair of shoes that are comfortable to stand in for a lengthy period of time. Avoid high heels when possible. They make a lot of noise and can be tricky to navigate. I once saw an influential female executive twist her ankle during a keynote address when her shoe's heel snapped off as she tripped over a computer cord. She delivered the rest of her talk from a stool with her foot on ice.

Finally, do a literal dress rehearsal. Practice delivering your presentation dressed in the attire in which you intend to present. In this way, you will not be distracted by your clothing when you present for real. For example, some speakers are surprised by how wearing a tie restricts their breathing, or others are flustered when their jacket's shoulder pads rise as they gesture broadly. The bottom line is that if you dress appropriately and comfortably, you will feel more confident and avoid distracting yourself and your audience.

Try this: Take time to determine an appropriate wardrobe for your presentation. Consider the expectations of your speaking situation and audience. You want to be comfortable in your appearance and avoid any distractions that your clothing or accessories might provide. Be sure to practice delivering your talk in your presentation clothes and shoes.

Finally, to overcome the initial spike of anxiety when you begin speaking, you should dedicate extra time to practicing the delivery of your talk's first 30 seconds. Going from silence to full presenting–also known as *commencing*–can be a tough transition that brings extra anxiety. You can practice starting smoothly by using some standard commencing line: Express gratitude for your speaking opportunity, comment on the person introducing you, or talk about the speaking occasion or venue. By having your first words prepared, you can use the time when you are delivering them to scan the room and get acquainted with your surroundings. Much like a football team that has its first few plays scripted, **planning out your commencing sentences** allows you to calm your nerves and gain your composure.

Sample commencing sentences:

▶ "Thank you for inviting me to present."
▶ "I appreciate the kind words that (name of introducer) shared with you."
▶ "I am really excited to be here at (name the venue/event)."

 Try this: Write your commencing sentences on a note card. Practice delivering these lines. Further, practice scanning around the room and looking at your audience.

Theory 2: Learning Theory

Remember Pavlov's famous experiment with his dogs? He trained them to salivate when he rang a bell because they thought they were going to get food. The dogs had learned to associate the stimulus of the bell ringing with the presentation of food. When applied to speaking anxiety, learning theory says that somehow you have learned to associate speaking in front of others as negative, bad, or nerve-wracking. Perhaps you learned to see speaking as anxiety provoking because you had a bad experience when you were younger, you heard that a friend or someone you care about had a bad experience, or you watched something negative happen in the media. In other words, through *conditioning*, some type of modeling caused you to think that speaking in front of others is a bad thing.

According to learning theory, the way to manage speaking anxiety is to extinguish this fear. *Extinguish* means to get rid of the conditioned association or to replace it with something else. The therapeutic management technique based on this theory is called **visualization**. If you've ever played a sport, your coach might have told you to visualize, to think about yourself doing whatever that sport requires–maybe kicking the ball into the goal, having the bat hit the ball, making the ball go into the basket. Research from sports psychology shows that the best way athletes can improve their skills is to practice. The second best way is to visualize. You can improve your skills, reduce your anxiety, and increase your confidence just by envisioning yourself speaking.

What would an extinguishing visualization be like? Say you're taking a speech class, and you are troubled by your anxiety level in the class. Here's a sample script that you might use to visualize being in that class. Once you have an idea of what this is like, you can tailor the script to work for you and your speaking situation.

> Imagine yourself having to give a presentation in your speech class. It is the morning of that presentation. You wake up. You feel refreshed. You had a good night's sleep. You feel good. You get dressed. You put

on clothes that fit right and make you look good. You feel confident. You go to the class. Traffic is smooth and perfect—no delays. You find an amazing parking space right where you want to be. You walk into the classroom. Your fellow students are ready. They're excited to see you. They're awake and engaged. When it's your turn to speak, you get up in front of your class. You're confident; you're sure of yourself. You know you will do a good job. As you're speaking, your audience pays attention. Everyone understands what you're saying. They're focused. At the end, they give you loud applause, and you know that you communicated your ideas clearly. Your audience understood your message. At the end of class, your teacher tells you, "Good job." You feel good about your performance. You know you did your best. (This script is a modified version of the one used in J. Ayers and T. Hopf's research).

Notice that during this visualization you didn't just focus on the speech. As a matter of fact, you didn't focus specifically on what you were saying at all. Sometimes, for nervous people, trying to relax and focus on what they are going to say makes them more nervous; this is called *relaxation-induced anxiety*. That's *not* the goal of visualization. You're trying to make yourself less nervous. What you do is focus holistically on your entire speaking experience, not on any one particular element of it, and try relaxing and see positive things happening.

An important key to making this work is to do the visualization days ahead, not just immediately before you speak. You need to do it several days in advance, once or twice a day, because you're getting yourself into a pattern. Remember, you're trying to extinguish and unlearn a long-held negative association and replace it with a positive one.

Try **Try this:** Identify a speaking opportunity several days from now. Three days before speaking, when you are in a calm and relaxed mood, take yourself through your own modified version of the visualization script (see the previous visualization script). Repeat this over the next two days. Note how you feel during the visualization and afterward. Further, note how your overall anxiety regarding the speaking abates.

Solutions-focused therapy provides another anxiety reduction technique that is similar to visualization in that it focuses on positive outcomes. Rather than envisioning a future presentation, solutions-focused therapy asks you to reflect on your successes in the past—no matter how small. For example, your introductory joke might have really been a big hit or you had your idea funded because of the value proposition you articulated. Once you have cataloged a few successes, you can analyze them for factors that led to their success. Was it that you were particularly passionate in your delivery? Did your ideas resonate strongly with your audience? Did you get a good night's sleep prior to presenting? Whatever your analysis reveals provides a starting point for you to expand in future presentations. By invoking this technique, you allow your successes, rather than your learned fears, to be your guide.

Try

> **Try this: Document your successes at present-ing.** Once you have delineated your successes, no matter how big or small, identify the factors that contributed to your success. What did you do, what didn't you do, was there something about the audi-ence or context that brought about your success? Once you have identified these factors, you can replicate them in your future preparation, practice, and performance.

Theory 3: Biological Theory

Biological theory suggests two explanations for why we experience anxiety: (1) You're made nervous by the onslaught of neurotransmitters and hormones that cre-ate and exacerbate your anxiety reaction, and (2) you're nervous when speaking in front of others because you have an excessive activation of your fear response.

Understand Neurotransmitters and Hormones

To begin, a symphony of chemicals called glucocor-ticoids, including cortisol and adrenaline, is released throughout your body when a threat, such as public speaking, presents itself. Some of these chemicals ini-tiate actions (e.g., increase heart rate), whereas others inhibit them (e.g., stop digestion). Pharmaceuticals have been around for a number of years that can short-circuit or block the action of fear-induced neurotransmitters and hormones. Medicines like beta-blockers, Valium, and certain classes of antidepressants can reduce some of the symptoms of anxiety. Yet these drugs are not without drawbacks; their use carries with it the risk of addiction, inability to concentrate, and reduced blood pressure. Interestingly, acetaminophen (found in Tylenol) has recently been shown to reduce the physio-logical manifestations of fear, but caution must be taken as there are many concerns about liver damage resulting from excess acetaminophen use.

Researchers have recently found that oxytocin, which promotes bonding between people, can reduce many of the symptoms of social anxiety. Unlike the pharmaceuticals mentioned above, plenty of oxytocin is produced in your body naturally. Every time you hug a friend, chat with a relative on the phone, shake hands, or kiss your spouse or child, your body releases oxytocin.

Try **Try this:** Prior to speaking, spend some time with a person on whom you can rely for social support. Perhaps you can walk to your presentation with this supportive person. Or, shake hands with some of your supportive audience members. These interactions will **release a burst of oxytocin** in your body, which can naturally reduce some of your speaking jitters.

Recent research has shown that acting courageous in the face of fear actually reduces the anxiety you feel. The neurotransmitters released when performing bravely blunt the impact of cortisol and adrenaline.

Try **Try this: Act courageously prior to speaking** to release neurotransmitters that will reduce your nervous symptoms caused by cortisol and adrenaline. You could volunteer to present first, ask a question of the previous speaker, or introduce the speaker who presents before you.

Address Excessive Activation

According to the second biological explanation for public speaking anxiety, people have different reactions to anxiety-provoking situations or stimuli. Some people are more sensitive, have a lower threshold, or respond more strongly than others. Think of it this way: You go to a movie with a friend and something scary happens on the screen. Your friend might almost jump out of her seat in fear, while your own response is minimal. You both saw the same thing, but you each reacted very differently. These personal differences exist for speaking anxiety.

The technique that addresses this biological mechanism is **systematic desensitization**, also known as exposure therapy. Systematic desensitization works to change unconscious associations between some aversive stimulus and your anxiety. It works like this: Over time you expose yourself repeatedly to the thing that makes you fearful, with each successive exposure becoming more real or immediate. Eventually, you get to a point where you can do the thing that frightens you–like flying, walking across a high bridge, or giving a speech–without being nervous.

To begin, systematic desensitization has you identify what happens in your body physiologically when you get nervous. What is the first physical sign of anxiety that you experience? A particular muscle group might tense up, you might start to feel queasy, or you might get a headache. Each person has his or her own physiological trigger that fires first when anxiety sets in. Systematic desensitization asks you to become sensitive to your physiological trigger so that when you begin to feel it, you can use relaxation techniques to short-circuit or stop the anxiety response.

 Try this: Take a minute to quiet your mind and relax your body. Closing your eyes and taking a few deep breaths should help. Once you feel calmer, think of a recent stressful event. Try to identify what happened first to your body when you began to think of the stressor. This response is likely your physi-ological trigger.

There are numerous relaxation techniques, such as deep breathing, yoga, a warm bath, chi gong, and the like. A simple, yet effective technique is **sequential muscle relaxation**. In this technique, you progressively tense groups of muscles in your body for a few seconds and then slowly release the tension. For example, start with your feet and then progress to your lower legs, upper legs, torso, and arms. By monitoring your breathing–holding your breath on the muscle contraction for two counts and releasing it slowly for two counts as you relax–you can significantly reduce your anxiety. Once you feel that physiological trigger, use your relaxation technique until you get to a point where you're relaxed.

Try **Try this:** While sitting or lying down, talk yourself through the sequential muscle relax-ation technique. Begin by tensing and relaxing your toes while monitoring your breathing. Work your way through your entire body until you are tens-ing and relaxing your forehead. When you're done with this exercise, you should feel more relaxed and notice that you're breathing more fully, calmly, and steadily.

Now, you're ready for the systematic desensitiza-tion. If you're trying to feel less nervous standing in front of a large audience giving a speech, you don't start by imagining the thing that makes you most nervous. You start small. So, imagine yourself simply writing a speech. You're not even writing; you're just imagining writing the speech. For many people who are anxious about speaking, this is enough to trigger a nervous reaction. You would immediately invoke your relaxation technique and repeat it until you can relax and get to a point where thinking about writing a speech does not trigger much nervousness. This might take an hour, a day, a week, a month, a year–it can take a long time.

Then, you systematically move to the next level that invokes anxiety, such as starting to write a speech. When the anxious feelings start, you again invoke your relaxation technique, repeating it until you can write the speech without feeling anxiety. Next, you might stand in front of a mirror and practice delivering the speech. Again, you would alleviate the anxiety via your relaxation practice. After a while, perhaps a long while, you will have short-circuited your exaggerated anxiety response and be able to get up in front of an audience and speak.

Systematic desensitization works. It's a powerful and effective technique. However, it takes time. Some professionals, such as therapists and speaking coaches, devote their practices solely to helping people through this exposure process.

Try → **Try this:** Identify five increasingly threatening steps in delivering a speech. Begin by relaxing yourself (see the previous "Try this"), and think about the least threatening of the steps you just identified. When you start feeling nervous, begin your relaxation practice. Repeat this process until you can envision the threat without having your trigger fire. You are now ready to begin again with the next threatening step you identified.

Theory 4: Cognitive Theory

Cognitive theory has four aspects to it: (1) framing, (2) negative self-talk, (3) repeated negative attributions, and (4) irrational thinking. Different techniques can be used to overcome each of these aspects.

Reframe the Situation

Many people see speaking as being like acting. When you perform, you have specific lines you need to speak in a certain way at an exact place. What happens when an actor doesn't say his or her lines at the right time or doesn't stand in the right place? It causes problems for the other actors and stagehands and creates confusion for the audience. In a performance, there is a right way and a wrong way. This performance anxiety is what causes many actors and actresses to get nervous. They know they could do something wrong.

Giving a speech is not performing. Many people think that it is. They think that there's a right way and a wrong way to give a speech, but there isn't. Certainly, there are better ways, but there is no one correct way. So, the first cognitive technique involves what psychologists call *reappraisal*, which in this case means *reframing* the speaking situation as a conversation rather than a performance. It's just a conversation where you do most of the talking. As in any conversation, your audience provides you with immediate and direct responses–albeit nonverbal feedback. Most people who get nervous about giving a speech do not get nervous when having a conversation about the same topic with their friends, coworkers, or family.

Let's say you're giving a pitch on why customers should buy your product. You could sit with your friends and talk about why they should purchase from you, and you would not be nervous. However, if you were asked to get up in front of prospective customers and talk about why they should buy your product, you might get very nervous. If you **reframe the situation as a conversation**, and not as a performance, you should be less anxious and more comfortable.

But how do you do this? Simply telling yourself, "Okay. I'm going to converse with you," isn't going to have much of an impact on your nervousness. First and foremost, you should *not* memorize your speech. Memorization is predicated on the assumption that there is a right way to say something (the way you memorized it). Rather, work on *extemporaneous speaking*, in which you practice speaking aloud from an outline of key points. Better yet, have the outline simply list your key points as questions. This type of question-based outline gets you prepared to be interactive because questions involve dialog. You might say these points differently each time, but you are still conveying your central arguments. Additionally, when you practice, don't stand up and deliver in front of a mirror or camera. Practice by sitting at a coffee table or at a coffee shop with friends or family to talk through your speech. Include the word "you" frequently when speaking. "You" provides a direct, verbal connection with your audience and leads to a more conversational tone and approach. You can also use audience members' names if you know them. When you converse, you connect with people through using their names. Finally, consider starting your presentation with a question to your audience. Questions—regardless of whether not they are rhetorical—are highly effective conversation starters. These techniques turn your practice and presentation into a conversation.

Activities to make your presentation conversational

- ▶ Speak extemporaneously from a bulleted outline.
- ▶ Practice in a conversational setting such as a dinner table.
- ▶ Use the word "you" frequently when referring to your audience.
- ▶ Mention the names of some of the people in your audience.
- ▶ Ask questions at the start of your presentation.

Try **Try this:** After you have collected your thoughts for a specific presentation and organized them in a coherent manner, invite a friend or two to sit with you and talk with them about your ideas. You are not presenting or performing. Rather, you are conversing.

Combat the Negative Self-Talk

Most people say a lot to themselves. Often, this intrapersonal dialog is negative: "You're going to screw up," "Your hair looks awful," "You're going to forget what you're saying." For those who suffer from speaking anxiety, these negative thoughts are both intrusive and pervasive. Beyond being annoying, these negative thoughts result in a *self-fulfilling prophecy*–you expect something is going to happen and it does, because you make it happen. Here's an example of how it works. You're about to give a speech. You say, "This is going to go poorly." This kind of a thought process increases your stress, resulting in a worse speech. By virtue of your negative self-talk, you have ensured a bad presentation.

The technique for reversing this vicious cycle is simply to replace negative comments with **positive affirmations**. Rather than saying, "I'm going to mess this up," you instead say, "This is a great opportunity to share my experience with my audience." Note that this affirmation is not unbelievably positive. It's not saying, "This is going to be the best speech ever!" It's just acknowledging the reality that you have a great opportunity to convey your ideas. When you think that you have a great opportunity, that makes you feel positive, which, in turn, makes you more relaxed. The more relaxed you are, the more likely you are to give a good presentation. You're using self-fulfilling prophecy to obtain a positive outcome, not a negative one.

Before you even prepare a presentation, you should create some positive affirmations that are relevant and meaningful to you. Then, before you speak, you can consciously say one of these affirmations. Affirmations should not be long sayings or contain too many concepts. Research on sports performance has found that simple, one-word mantras (e.g., *focus*, *calm*, *fun*) confer benefits because they eliminate overthinking and reduce negative self-fulfilling prophecies. If you are struggling to come up with useful affirmations, you can focus on values that are important to you, such as education (e.g., "I will teach people something of value during my talk."), fairness (e.g., "It's my turn to share my thoughts."), and similar ideas.

<u>Sample positive affirmations</u>

- ▶ People will listen politely to my ideas.
- ▶ My audience will learn something of value from me.
- ▶ I have presented well on this topic before.
- ▶ I can handle this.
- ▶ Enthusiasm.
- ▶ Connection.

Try

Try this: Create a positive affirmation that is meaningful to you. Be sure that your affirmation is short, memorable, and reasonable. Rehearse it aloud. You will be empowered by hearing the affirmation. Be sure to say this affirmation before a presentation. Make it the last thing you say to yourself before you begin to speak.

Playing off this notion of positive affirmation, research has shown that **optimism helps reduce anxiety**. You can leverage this benefit in two ways: First, you can look on the bright side beyond your speaking situation. Contemplate positive events after you present. For example, if you are presenting during a meal, you can think about the nice chocolate dessert you will enjoy after you speak. Further, you can envision some fun activity you will enjoy on the weekend after your Friday corporate all-hands presentation you're delivering. Second, you can look at your speaking event as a glass that is half full. Most nervous speakers see a presentation as a threatening situation that must be endured. Be optimistic and envision your presentation as a great opportunity.

Envisioning enjoyable, desired future activities and seeing speaking as a positive opportunity should help reduce your anxiety in the present moment.

Try **Try this:** Generate a list of things that you can look forward to after you present. These can be activities or items. By imagining future optimistic outcomes unrelated to and beyond your presentation, you will be less anxious during the presentation.

Distance Yourself from Your Fear

An *attribution* is an explanation for why things happen. If you're anxious about an upcoming presentation, you will often think very negatively about yourself and the whole speaking situation. You might begin to forecast your failure by explaining why you're going to do poorly: "I didn't get a good night's sleep," "I really didn't do enough research," "I didn't have enough time to prepare." You have all these excuses and justifications for why you're going to fail before you even have an opportunity to fail. And since it's very easy to live up to your lowest expectations, how you think leads to your failure.

A useful technique to break this cycle of negative attributions comes from being mindful. Among many other things, **mindfulness** increases cognitive flexibility and capability. It also teaches you how to nonjudgmentally observe yourself thinking and feeling, which allows you to be more comfortable and able to focus on your presentation. This approach can help reduce the need to explain away your potential failure, put things into perspective, and calm your anxiety. When you are feeling negative or nervous about speaking, say to yourself, "This is me feeling nervous about speaking." This kind of assertion takes you out of the nervousness and instead allows you to observe yourself being nervous. To be outside yourself affords you the opportunity to calm down. You can gain a sense of control. Further, by thinking of a positive emotion—such as calmness or happiness—once you have distanced yourself from your negative feelings, you will more quickly reduce your feelings of anxiety.

You can do the same thing when you're experiencing any charged emotion. Say you're feeling nervous, angry, or jealous. Just take a moment and say, "This is me feeling that way." That little reflective space between you and your feelings allows you to ask, "Okay, now what do I do?" This technique enables you to ask yourself helpful questions rather than living in the anxiety, anger, or jealousy.

Try **Try this:** Practice distancing yourself from your emotions. Think of a recent emotional event, positive or negative. While you reexperience the emotion, consciously tell yourself, "This is me feeling X emotion." Experience the space this gives you. Notice that you can think about and evaluate your feelings and responses more clearly.

Think about It Rationally

Cognitive modification techniques address the irrational nature of our speaking fears. If you think for a moment about the worst thing that could happen to you when speaking in public, you will realize that it isn't really that awful. What is absolutely the worst thing that could happen? You might forget your presentation. Other people might think you're unprepared. Maybe people will laugh at you. The first thing to realize is that you have had moments when bad things have happened. Who hasn't done something foolish? Who hasn't been laughed at or forgotten something important? The key is: You survived! You weren't happy about it. You may have felt bad. You might have had to make some life changes. But you're still here, often better off than before.

Next, think about the likelihood that your worst fear will come true. If you're afraid of forgetting your speech–that you'll be on the spot with nothing to say–what is the likelihood (from 0 to 100 percent) of that happening? A 100-percent certainty means it's absolutely going to happen, and 0 percent means it's not. When you think about your fear in this way, you will realize that it's a bit irrational. The likelihood of your fear coming true is not equal to the enormity of your fear reaction. **Being rational and recognizing your resilience** in the face of negative outcomes represent another aspect of the cognitive theory of anxiety management.

Try

Try this: Take a minute or two to write down all the fears that come to mind when you know you must give a public speech. On the top of a blank page, write "When I present, I am afraid that:". Then, list as many fears as you can, regardless of how silly or strange they may seem. (For example, "I'm afraid I'll forget my speech.") Next, write down (1) the worst thing that could happen to you personally and to the audience if the specific fear came true and (2) the likelihood (as a percentage) of this fear coming true for you in your next speech. (For example, "I'll embarrass myself, and the audience will feel awkward and laugh at me." "There is a 10 percent chance that I will forget my speech.") Reflect on what you have written. Notice that your fears, while real, are often not imminent or even highly likely. And even if they are, the result of their coming true would not be devastating.

Finally, the mere act of **writing down your fears** and concerns has been shown to reduce a wide range of performance anxieties—from test taking to sports performance to presenting. Similarly, **verbally stating how your fear is making you feel** can reduce your fear. Putting your fears on paper or speaking them out loud offloads them. Further, by making them explicit, your fears become less personal. In essence, they become "the" fears, not "your" fears. The words you use to describe the experience of your fears influences the effect writing about them has. When writing about your anxiety over a past presentation and its effects on you, use the past tense. For example, "I forgot my second point" versus "I keep forgetting my points." Additionally, the more negative words you use to describe how you are feeling, the greater the anxiety reduction. For example, "I am *terrified* of that *scary* speaking situation where I am *likely to forget* my points and *embarrass* myself in front of my colleagues." Research suggests that if you include some self-affirming comments in your writing and speaking about your fears, you can further lower your anxiety response. At the end of your list of fears, writing statements, such as "even with these fears, I will do my best" or "despite having these concerns, I will do justice to my topic," will help you feel more confident.

Try **Try this:** Write or speak out loud your concerns and fears of presenting. Provide a detailed description of the negative feelings you have, but conclude with at least one self-affirming statement.

Theory 5: Evolutionary Theory

According to evolutionary theory, you're anxious because you're worried about the consequences of what you're doing. You're preoccupied with getting an A in class, getting the job, closing the deal, or embarrassing yourself. These are all things that could happen in the future, after you've spoken.

A fundamental tenet of evolution is that status is important. Status refers to your position in a social hierarchy. Ten thousand years ago, when human beings were evolving, possessing high status gave an individual access to the fundamental necessities of survival, such as shelter, sexual partners, and food. In other words, possessing higher status increased the likelihood of survival. Conversely, having low status back then decreased access to essential resources and, thus, the likelihood that a person would survive.

Since speaking in front of others is fraught with potentially negative future outcomes, evolutionary psychologists suggest that social anxiety (of which public speaking anxiety is a major component) is adaptive for humans. In other words, your evolutionarily ingrained concern for your social status leads you to constantly evaluate your status compared to others and to worry about the consequences of behavior that might risk your status. Speaking in public represents a very salient threat to your status.

How do you undo this constant evaluation and innate fear? Before speaking, **focus on the present** and avoid thinking about the consequences of your actions. Having a present-oriented experience, sometimes referred to as a flow experience, savoring, or rapt attention, means you're so involved in the present that you lose track of time, external stimuli, and your overall self-awareness. Being focused on the present distracts you from the source of your nervousness and reduces the anxious arousal. You have likely had moments of extreme present orientation in certain situations, like when you play a sport or musical instrument, or when you engage in a deep conversation with a loved one.

Many techniques are available to help you to become more present oriented. Being physical is one technique. I know a professional speaker who deals with his nervousness by doing 100 pushups immediately before he speaks. After this speaker completes his pushups, he jumps up and then steps on the stage to speak. He carries his present orientation with him, along with a little sweat and tingling shoulder muscles. When you're challenging yourself physically, it's hard to think about the future. I know of another professional speaker who plays a handheld video game immediately before presenting. She sets her watch alarm for the time her speech is to begin and then plays a game like Tetris, which is very engaging. She becomes so involved in playing the game–very present oriented–that she is surprised when the alarm goes off. She simply turns off the device and walks on stage to speak.

Listening to music can also help induce a present-oriented perspective. Find a song or a play list that is engaging for you and practice becoming absorbed in it. Using humor can also be a fun way to become present oriented. Watch a funny video clip, listen to a comedy routine, or engage in a humorous exchange. Enjoying a good laugh often involves being highly in the moment.

Counting backward or saying tongue twisters are other ways to avoid future thinking before you speak. Counting backward requires astute attention to do it right. Additionally, it is nearly impossible to say a tongue twister accurately and not be fully engaged and present oriented. Not only can doing these last two suggestions make you less anxious about speaking, but if you do them out loud, they help you warm up your vocal cords for speaking.

Activities to become present oriented immediately prior to speaking

▶ Listen to music you enjoy.
▶ Engage in mildly intense physical activity.
▶ Watch, read, or listen to something funny.
▶ Count backward.
▶ Repeat tongue twisters.

A much more advanced technique for becoming present oriented is used by some politicians who often give the same speech over and over again but still get nervous. A politician will find someone to give her two random words, such as "green" and "bicycle." She will then work these words into her standard presentation in such a way that it doesn't seem strange. She won't get up and say, "Thank you for coming today green bicycles. We're going to..." Rather, she will fold these novel, unrelated words into her normal presentation. Think about what this forces her to do. She has to really focus on what she is saying. She has to be incredibly present oriented.

The ability to live in the moment and not worry about future consequences can be enjoyable, and it can be quite practical. Most adults, however, are future oriented. Thus, the trick lies in practicing techniques that enable you to move into a more present-oriented state when the situation requires it.

Try **Try this:** Repeat the following tongue twister aloud three times: "I slit a sheet. A sheet I slit. And on that slitted sheet I sit." If you say it wrong, you say a naughty word. When you were saying it, you probably couldn't focus on anything else. You were very present oriented.

Key Take Aways

- Dedicating time to learning about and actually delivering presentations helps build confidence. This benefit increases if you do this practice in a supportive and encouraging environment (e.g., classes or Toastmasters).
- Taking deep, sustained breaths helps reduce physiological anxiety symptoms as well as supports your voice and volume.
- Desensitize yourself so your speaking situation is less novel and more in your control. Visualization, gradual exposure, and rehearsing in your actual speaking environment can help.
- Reframe your presentation as a conversation. Avoid memorizing by using an outline rather than a manuscript.
- Be present oriented to avoid worrying about potential consequences.

AcTivity

Reflect on a recent speaking event. When things went well, what supported this positive outcome? When things did not go as well as you had hoped, what led to this outcome?

In your reflection, please consider the following:

- Who your audience was (did you know them, were they knowledgeable on your topic, had you presenting in front of them before?)
- Your mode of delivery (in person, via the web, standing, seated, etc.)
- Content you covered (was it new to you, did you write an outline, did you have a manuscript, did you use slides?)
- Context in which you presented (was this a large room, how were the seats configured, what time of day was it?)
- Your preparation (did you practice out loud, did you check out the room prior to speaking?)
- Interaction/involvement of the audience (did you ask questions during your presentation, did you use stories that were relevant to your audience?)
- Speaking hygiene (did you eat well prior to speaking, did you get a good night's rest, did you have caffeine before speaking?).

_____

_____

_____

_____

_____

_____

_____

_____

_____

_____

_____

CHAPTER 3
Audience Focus and Connection

ANXIETY REDUCTION VIA AUDIENCE CONNECTION

While your speaking anxiety resides within you, it is often made worse by the interaction–or lack of interaction–you have with your audience. To begin, an anxious speaker often makes his or her audience uncomfortable. It is not easy to watch someone struggle while presenting. Since most audiences are comprised of kind people who want the speaker to succeed, they enact behaviors that they think will help a nervous speaker gain composure and calm down, such as avert their gaze, distract themselves by looking at their phones, or chat with each other. Unfortunately, a nervous speaker witnessing these benevolent audience behaviors views the audience as disengaged and uninvolved, which only makes the speaker more nervous. The best way to avoid this awkward, anxiety-induced audience situation is to real-ize that your primary job as a speaker is to make your audience comfortable. If they are comfortable, they can pay attention and connect to you and your content.

In order to make your audience comfortable, you must break an insidious assumption that most speakers make. Many speakers assume that giving a presentation is about them as speakers. When you prepare a pre-sentation from your perspective, you likely pass over critical bits of information and fail to pull your audience into the content. Others label this self-focused approach "the curse of knowledge." Simply put, you often know too much about what you present. A better, more thor-ough approach to your presentation is to begin by focusing on the audience. Competent speakers never ask themselves, "What do I want to say?" Instead, they ask, "What does my audience need to hear or learn?" These two questions might sound similar, but they are very different. By focusing on your audience's needs, you remove yourself from the spotlight. Your audi-ence's needs are paramount. In taking this **audience-focused perspective**, nervous speakers can breathe a sigh of relief because failure is not related solely to them. If failure does occur, it results from the interaction between the audience and the topic. Additionally, by embracing an audience-focused approach, you not only engage your audience more—since you're giving them what they need—but you will present content that scaf-folds their knowledge so that they can truly appreciate and understand your message. Taken all together, this approach allows your audience to be more confortable and, thus, receive your message more readily.

I worked with a fantastic third-grade teacher who was incredibly confident and engaging when she was presenting to her students, but when asked to speak in front of adults, she became paralyzed by her fear. I asked her what made her a successful teacher. She quickly responded that she understands the needs of her students and makes sure to present her concepts in a way that meets those needs. We then spent some time extrapolating this simple recipe for her teaching success to her adult audiences. Her epiphany came when she realized that she needed to focus on the needs of her grownup audiences, just as she does with her 8-year-olds. By refocusing, she was able to contain her anxiety and release her passion. In fact, rather than being anxious about presenting to adults, she is now excited to present to them—she enjoys it now.

The audience-centric approach does require some extra work. You have to truly know your audience. Ask yourself the following three questions to help you better determine your audience's needs:

- What knowledge and/or past experience(s) have my audience had with my topic?
- What attitudes and emotions will my audience likely have toward my topic?
- What areas of resistance will my audience likely have toward my topic?

The answers to these three questions help you to develop and deliver a presentation that fulfills the needs of your audience, reduces your anxiety, and makes your message more compelling.

Try **Try this:** Think about your presentation topic. Ask yourself, "What does my audience need to know about the topic?" and "How can I ensure that they get the information they need?" The answers to these two questions move the spotlight away from you and put it on your audience.

Beyond being audience-centric and making your audience comfortable, your next goal when presenting is to pull your audience forward in their seats. You want them engaged and with you. Clearly, addressing their needs will help make your content compelling, but this is not sufficient. If you truly want your content to move your audience and avoid slouching disengagement, then you must make use of what I term Audience-Connecting Techniques (ACTs). ACTs bring your audience into your presentation. **ACTs invite their participation and serve notice that you expect engagement**. While many ACTs exist, the following techniques are among the most effective:

One easy to use ACT is to **ask your audience to participate**. For example, "With a show of hands, how many of you have:" or asking "which side of my slide best represents your experience?" Requests such as these show your audience that they are involved in your presentation.

Another useful ACT is to **ask your audience to visualize a situation or outcome.** For example, you can ask your audience to "imagine what it would be like if:" or "remember back to a time when:." Since your audience is seeing something in their mind's eye, rather than just listening to you describe it, they become more engaged and your point becomes more vivid and lasting for them.

Possibly the most important ACT is to **focus on the relevance of your topic for your audience.** Helping your audience to see the value of your topic to them is critical to engaging them. Be sure to spend time detailing the specific links between your topic and your audience's lives. You can signal this relevance with key phrases such as "the bottom line for you is:" or "what's important to remember is:." Relevancy is the best antidote for apathy, and it brings with it a high level of participation.

Try this: To help you remember to drive home the relevance of your points, focus on the key takeaway(s) for your audience. At the end of each major point you make, think to yourself how you would end the sentence: "The bottom line for you is:." While you might not actually speak these lines at the end of each of your points, you will be sure to focus on each point's relevance to your audience, which in turn, will make you more confident because you will know that they are getting what they need from your presentation.

Another helpful ACT is **Think-Pair-Share**. Ask your audience to take a moment to think of an answer to a question you pose or to come up with a potential alternative. Next, encourage them to discuss their response with someone near them. After this brief discussion, solicit their input. Think-Pair-Share is a powerful participation tool because it not only bolsters the audience's confidence in responding because they have collaborated on their response, but better ideas typically arise as a result of multiple brains working together.

A final ACT is to **step toward your audience when you begin your presentation.** Since most speakers experience some degree of anxiety when presenting, they often hide behind a lectern or place their hands up in front of their bodies leaning back away from the audience. As discussed in Chapter 1, this nonverbal retreating position signals fear and invites disengagement. Rather, as you begin, stand tall in front of the audience—no podium in sight–and step forward with your arms extended away from your body. A start like this nonverbally communicates confidence and demonstrates that you want your audience involved.

Try **Try this:** Identify two **Audience-Connecting Techniques** from those mentioned above that you feel most comfortable using. Think of a number of ways to invoke the ACTs you selected in your next presentation.

Nowhere are the audience-centric approach and audience-connecting techniques more salient and useful than in the **introduction to your presentation**. The purpose of the introduction is threefold. First, an introduction must capture your audience's focus. Second, it has to quickly explain the relevance and significance of your topic or position to your audience. You must answer the tandem questions of "So what?" and "Why should you care?" Finally, your introduction needs to set your audience's expectations for what is to come. The most effective way to fulfill your introduction's first purpose is to use an audience-connecting technique, such as asking a polling question (e.g., "How many of you have ever been frustrated by:?"). Any audience-connecting technique helps your audience to focus on you and your message. These techniques pull your audience into your presentation. Once you have your audience engaged, you must explain why your topic is relevant and important to them. You need to state your speaking purpose (i.e., sometimes called a thesis statement) in one clear, declarative sentence framed from your audience's perspective. With your audience's attention focused and their understanding of the value of what you intend to say, you now conclude your introduction by highlighting what is to follow.

When you focus on your audience and use audience-connecting techniques throughout your presentation, but especially in your introduction, you reap many benefits: (a) Your audience feels more connected to your content, (b) your audience will be more comfortable and ready to listen, and (c) you will feel less anxious because you and your audience are actively working together.

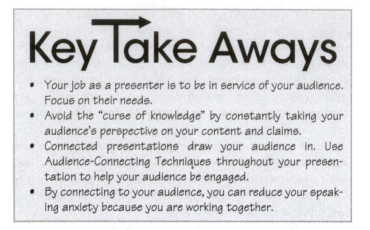

Key Take Aways

- Your job as a presenter is to be in service of your audience. Focus on their needs.
- Avoid the "curse of knowledge" by constantly taking your audience's perspective on your content and claims.
- Connected presentations draw your audience in. Use Audience-Connecting Techniques throughout your presentation to help your audience be engaged.
- By connecting to your audience, you can reduce your speaking anxiety because you are working together.

AcTivity

For an upcoming presentation, analyze your audience and their needs by answering the following questions:

- What are my audience's expectations of my presentation?
- Has my audience heard a presentation similar to mine before? What worked and didn't with this prior presentation?
- What does my audience know about my topic and position?
- What are my audience's attitudes toward my topic and position?
- What areas of concern or resistance might my audience have?

_____

_____

_____

_____

_____

_____

_____

_____

_____

_____

CHAPTER 4
Memory, Speaking Hygiene, and Structure

HOW CAN YOU AVOID BLANKING OUT?

Memory is an important consideration in any discussion of communication apprehension. Many people say their biggest speaking fear is forgetting what they are going to say or exactly how they want to say something. Memory research can teach you a lot about good mental hygiene for speaking.

Eat, Be Fit, and Sleep Well

The first piece of advice sounds like something a parent might suggest: Eat healthfully, be fit, and sleep well. Unfortunately, healthful eating often goes out the window when a speaking deadline is fast approaching. However, paying attention to your diet can help alleviate your anxiety as well as improve your memory.

Here is a bit of consumption advice: Simple sugars and sweets provide a quick energy boost, which is often followed by sluggishness. Complex carbohydrates, nuts, omega-3 fatty acids, flavanols (found in grapes, berries, apples, and cocoa), and oils help in memory formation and retention. So, like a long-distance runner, you might find it helpful to carbo-load when preparing a presentation. Caffeine facilitates creativity and productivity, but it also invites jitters, dry mouth, and flighty memory. It makes sense to go for the triple mocha latte when preparing a speech, but it's not a good idea just before presenting it. Remember: The effects of caffeine linger in the body for a number of hours. Although alcohol might be tempting as a relaxation tool, evidence suggests it causes forgetfulness and "loosens the tongue," which might lead to regret. Finally, recent research suggests that probiotic bacteria found in many "live culture" yogurts lower the levels of stress-inducing hormones.

Try **Try this: Create a meal plan** or menu that itemizes the food and drink you will consume before writing, preparing, and presenting your speech. Have this food and drink handy so that you won't be tempted to indulge in things that might cause problems for you.

Exercise plays an important role in both memory and anxiety resilience. Exercise physiologists and psychologists have found that people with lower percentages of body fat and lower average resting heart rates handle stressful situations better than those who are not as fit. In-shape presenters respond better to both the cognitive and the physiological aspects of stress. Additionally, physical activity increases lung capacity and bolsters mental focus, two very important aspects of speech delivery. Short, intense bursts of exercise that follow new learning have been shown to increase remembering. Finally, exercise provides an avenue for releasing pent-up anxiety and stress. Try to go for a quick swim, jog, or walk prior to writing or practicing a speech. The calming effect that results comes not just from getting outside and distancing yourself from the stressor, but also from your body's natural endorphins, which are often released when you exercise. Memory research clearly shows that the less stressed you are, the more information you will retain.

Try this: Create an exercise plan that gets you moving. Before working on your presentation, take 20 minutes to enjoy your exercise plan. Note how much calmer you are, and observe how much sharper you feel mentally after you are done exercising.

With your stomach full, your body fit, and your mind primed to remember, sleep becomes the next important area to examine. Although much remains unknown about sleep, research shows that good-quality, deep sleep is involved in memory formation, especially when you sleep shortly after learning occurs. Further, sleep helps with creativity and energy. A good night's sleep helps prepare the brain for learning and consolidates newly learned memories so that you can recall them more easily. When you are authoring and preparing a speech, try to **get a full night's sleep** rather than pulling an all-nighter.

Try

Try this: When authoring and practicing a speech, be sure to go to bed and wake up at your regular times. Avoid altering your sleep-wake schedule. If you find yourself ruminating over your presentation while trying to fall asleep, keep a notebook by your pillow so that you can write down your thoughts and release their hold on you.

Play can also be a powerful tool to alleviate stress and refresh your energy. Consciously make time to play with your pet, children, or friends. Even short bursts of play can sharpen your mind and improve your spirits.

Memory and Location

The location where you practice your presentation should be similar to where you will present it. This concept is called *state—dependent learning.* The context in which you learn helps you remember. For example, if you are going to take an exam in a quiet room, you should study in a quiet room. If you are going to give a speech in a large room with big windows where people are quiet and attentive, you should practice giving the speech in a large room with windows. Practicing in the place where you're presenting—or at least in a similar place—will facilitate your remembering. This advice also works for presenting via the web or teleconference. You can practice in the room with the technology that you will be using. In fact, practicing with the technology in advance is *always* a good idea.

Try

Try this: Reflect on the characteristics of the room in which you will be presenting. Better yet, go explore it if you can. When you prepare and practice your presentation, try to do so in a room similar in design, noise level, brightness, and the like.

Variety, Timing, and Testing

Over the past decade, memory researchers have been challenging commonly held notions of the best way to study and remember. Researchers are finding that, instead of relying on lengthy cramming sessions, taking breaks while learning and varying what you study aids in remembering. Further, self-testing appears more effective than mere repetition. For speakers, this new research suggests that you should focus on learning the content of your speech in multiple blocks of time—say 20 minutes each—with breaks in between. Breaks involving wakeful rest, such as silent day dreaming, seem most effective. These breaks appear to be helpful in long-term memory formation. Retention is increased by varying the content you learn because variety activates more brain regions. Thus, while learning, you should practice different portions of your speech, rather than fixating on one part until it becomes engrained. Finally, rather than simply saying your speech multiple times, you should test your recall of your content by asking yourself questions, such as "What is my central message?" and "How do I support my third claim?" Testing yourself in this fashion requires more cognitive effort and leads to deeper retention of the information.

Try **Try this: Create a content learning plan** that includes blocks of study time, varied parts of your presentation to learn, and specific questions that you can use to test how well you are remembering your content.

What Happens When You Do Blank Out?

All of the advice about eating, exercising, sleeping, and practicing can't guarantee that you won't forget something that you intended to say. So what can you do if and when you blank out? First, try not to be too hard on yourself. Often, speakers who forget blurt out comments that reduce their credibility: "Sheesh, how could I forget?," "I'm so nervous," or "I can't believe how stupid I am!" If you must overtly acknowledge your forgetfulness, simply apologize and collect your thoughts. One of my students once addressed her forgetfulness by simply saying to her audience: "You'll have to excuse me, but I am so passionate about my topic that I sometimes get ahead of myself. Allow me to review my previous point." Most audiences are very forgiving, and some may actually be thankful for the pause because it allows them time to process what you've presented.

To help get yourself back on track, focus on what you've just said. Too often, people who blank out try to figure out what they need to say next. You are more likely to continue smoothly if you reorient yourself by looking to what you said previously. The following techniques can help you get past a memory block: (1) Paraphrase your previous content. (2) Ask your audience a question-it can be rhetorical: "What seems to be the most important point so far?" (3) Review your overall speaking purpose: "So we can see that <insert your core message> is really important."

Structure Sets You Free

A powerful way to help both you and your audience remember your presentation is to **provide a meaningful structure to your content**. Research shows that people retain structured information up to 40 percent more reliably and accurately than information that is presented in an unstructured manner. Having your content structured helps you remember what you plan to say because even if you forget the specifics, you know the general structure. For example, when using the problem-solution-benefit structure, you first lay out a specific problem (or opportunity), and then you detail a solution to address the problem before defining the benefits to your solution. If you are in the middle of the solution part and you blank out, then by simply thinking back to your structure, you know that the benefits portion comes next. Another very useful structure that can help in many planned as well as spontaneous speaking situations (e.g., question-and-answer sessions) is the What?-So What?-Now What? structure. When using this structure, you start with your central claim (What?), then explain its importance or value (So What?) before concluding with a call to action or next steps (Now What?).

From the audience's perspective, your structure, especially if it is revealed up front in the form of a preview in your introduction, provides a roadmap for your presentation. Think of yourself as a tour guide whose number one goal is not to lose your tour group. As a vigilant tour guide, your job is to set your group's expectations for where they are going and how they will get there. These tasks are identical to what you must do for your audience. Once prepared by knowing your structure, your audience can focus comfortably on your content.

Try → **Try this:** Use a structure for your content. Consider your goal and presentation plan. Determine a structure to assist you and your audience in remembering your presentation.

In conclusion, eating properly, exercising, sleeping well, employing a structure for your content, and using the latest tips from memory research will enable you to increase your confidence, reduce your anxiety, and improve your memory. However, if you do blank out, there are techniques to help you quickly recover and keep your audience with you.

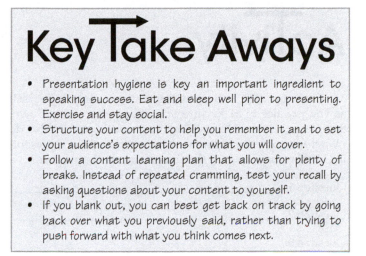

Key Take Aways

- Presentation hygiene is key an important ingredient to speaking success. Eat and sleep well prior to presenting. Exercise and stay social.
- Structure your content to help you remember it and to set your audience's expectations for what you will cover.
- Follow a content learning plan that allows for plenty of breaks. Instead of repeated cramming, test your recall by asking questions about your content to yourself.
- If you blank out, you can best get back on track by going back over what you previously said, rather than trying to push forward with what you think comes next.

AcTivity

Come up with five questions that you can ask yourself as you practice to make sure you have your content down. Sample questions include: What is my central point? What do I want my audience to know or do when I am done presenting? What story can I tell that best supports my purpose?

Question 1: _____

Question 2: _____

Question 3: _____

Question 4: _____

Question 5: _____

CHAPTER 5
Behaviors to Avoid

PROCRASTINATION, PRACTICE, PERFECTIONISM, AND POWERPOINT

Any discussion of speech anxiety would be incomplete without some mention of four common issues that tend to make speaking anxiety worse: procrastination, incomplete practice, perfectionism, and PowerPoint.

Procrastination

Procrastination refers to the conscious choice to put off your work. When this choice of inaction or distraction relates to speech making, it often increases anxiety. In other words, procrastination is short-term aversive mood reduction. Here's a typical anxiety-inducing cycle: Nervous people know that speech writing and presenting make them anxious, so they put off creating their speeches until the last minute. They don't want to experience the nervousness, and it's easier to put off the work or to become distracted than to confront the task and experience the fear. What is going to happen to people like this? At the last possible moment, they will begin to write their speech with very little time available. Thus, they have created a situation that provides them little time to refine their presentation, let alone practice it. Beyond creating a speech that falls short of its potential, this procrastination invites spikes in anxiety, not to mention feelings of helplessness and unnecessary guilt from knowing they could have (and should have) prepared earlier. Ultimately, procrastination leads to increased nervousness.

In addition to thinking that delay reduces their anxiety, procrastinators may think they gain a face-saving excuse. If they procrastinate and deliver a less-than-stellar speech, they can always tell themselves, "Well, if I had spent more time, it would have gone better." This built-in excuse only reinforces this vicious, nonproductive cycle.

The trick to avoiding procrastination is to **put yourself on a regular schedule**. Identify your presentation delivery date and map backward to determine your major deliverables. Here are some suggested timeframes. Give yourself three to four full days to practice your presentation. This means it needs to be completed almost a full work week before your delivery date. To achieve this practice period, you need to allow yourself at least five days to author the content (as mentioned previously, I recommend writing an outline only). You may need to add more time if you require research or rely on others for help (e.g., for information, to review your content, or to create accompanying visuals). That means you need at least 10 days to two weeks of working time before your delivery date. Mark all dates on your calendar. Manage your time so that you meet your deadlines. If it helps, create incentives for yourself for every milestone achieved. Further, sharing your goal(s) with others can gain you the support you might need to keep going forward. Post your plan on your refrigerator at home or near your office desk. Simply put, the fix for procrastination is planned preparation—what academics call *implementation intentions*. Taking control of your presentation preparation in this manner will bring about better presentations, deeper confidence, and less stress.

Try

Try this: Identify three incentives that motivate you. This could be anything from getting a massage to playing a video game to calling a friend. Use these incentives as rewards for accomplishing the itemized presentation milestones you have chosen for yourself.

Practice

As just mentioned in the discussion of procrastination, making time to practice is critical to feeling more confident and less nervous. However, many presenters don't practice properly. They simply mentally rehearse or flip through a slide deck. This approach is limited in its benefit. To practice effectively, you also need to stand and deliver. Rather than only thinking through a presentation, standing up and practicing your speech helps you remember it. Specifically, hearing your own voice and using relevant, appropriate gestures improve later recall. Thus, thinking about and speaking your presentation are the keys to successful practice. You benefit as a result of augmented memory consolidation because your mental imagery and physical practice use overlapping neural networks in your brain.

One very useful practice technique called **focused practice** involves taking one aspect of your presentation—say, the introduction—and delivering it repeatedly until you become highly familiar and comfortable with it (*Note:* Again, this does not mean you should memorize your presentation.). Next, you would move on to another aspect of your presentation, such as transitioning between two specific visual aids. Your repetitive practice leads to what psychologists call *overlearning*. Overlearning lessens your mental load because your practice has caused the material to become more automated. Ultimately, you feel more comfortable because you do not have to spend valuable mental effort thinking about all the particular aspects of your presentation.

Try **Try this:** To engage in focused practice, "chunk" your presentation into logical units, such as introduction, conclusion, point 1, transitions, etc. Practice each part separately until you feel comfortable and more relaxed with it. Chunking makes your practice and anxiety much more manageable.

Perfectionism

When perfectionism is harnessed appropriately, perfectionists or perfectionistic-leaning speakers with their ability to plan, prepare, and strive for success serve as incredibly valuable personal assets. These traits often lead to quality presentations with a manageable level of anxiety. Unfortunately, these beneficial characteristics, when taken to the extreme of perfectionism, can create more speaking anxiety and trouble. Since perfectionists set incredibly high standards for themselves and their work, they become easily discouraged when they fail to meet them. This sense of failure can paralyze perfectionists and make them reluctant to complete speaking preparation. The need to get it right comes with a huge fear of failing. This fear is made worse in speaking situations because perfectionists tend to worry about all of things that can go wrong in the speaking context over which they have little or no control. Wanting everything to be just right makes them worry about everything.

Because perfectionists worry about all the possible things that can go wrong, many suffer from "analysis paralysis," which limits the amount of time available for preparing and practicing the presentation. Anxiety research suggests that **planning for contingencies**, or alternate possible outcomes, can alleviate this restricting situation. In other words, be prepared so that if something goes wrong, you're ready and won't get flustered. It's like the fire safety plan you should have at home: If there's a fire, you know where to go to meet up with your loved ones. If your presentation relies on PowerPoint, and the projector doesn't work, what do you do? Do you panic? Or do you invoke your contingency plan and distribute the handouts you brought? What if you blank out during a transition? Do you walk away from the podium? Or do you simply glance down at your bulleted list of points on your note card? A plan affords you some piece of mind, allowing you to be less nervous and more focused. Ultimately, you will have a greater sense of control.

Try   **Try this:** Identify three to five situations that could cause you difficulty when you present. Think of problems related to your presentation, your materials, or the environment in which you speak. For example, what if the room is too warm or you need an extension cord? With these potential problems in mind, develop an action plan for each one. Remember to allow extra time to address these potential problems.

PowerPoint

The greatest presentation helper ever developed can also be the biggest roadblock to effective, low-anxiety presentations. When used well, Microsoft's PowerPoint and all the other visual presentation tools (e.g., Keynote, Prezi, Slide Rocket) facilitate understanding and let audiences absorb information in wonderful ways. Unfortunately, these tools can also enhance anxiety and often lead to poor presentations. Remember, PowerPoint is not the presentation. Your content and delivery are the presentation. PowerPoint is merely a tool. Far too often, speakers think they are writing a speech when they are only drafting PowerPoint slides. These two acts are different. If you were a pastry chef, it would be akin to spending hours icing a cake without regard for the quality of the cake itself. You must break this association. You write, practice, deliver, and are ultimately evaluated on the presentation you deliver, not on the slides you create. Also, not every speech lends itself to PowerPoint. To see this exemplified, search the Internet for Lincoln's "Gettysburg Address" as a PowerPoint. The power and beauty of this famous oration are stripped away completely when forced into the restrictive confines of PowerPoint.

From an anxiety perspective, creating PowerPoint slides gives you the illusion that you are making progress in crafting your speech. In fact, you are simply creating a glorified outline. Although outlines are incredibly valuable, the time spent creating slides is often orders of magnitude longer. The result is that you spend so much time creating slides with wipes, fades, and embedded videos that you fail to practice your presentation, and you lose your focus on delivering the message that your audience needs to hear. This all-to-common practice leads presenters to read their slides rather than connect with their audience. Your slides are a tool for engagement, not a teleprompter.

Tangentially, research suggests that being in a dark environment—much like the dimmed conference room or classroom needed for slides to project properly—increases anxiety. You and your audience might be better served to reduce the number of slides and **present in a well-lit room**.

It's not that you should avoid PowerPoint and the like. Rather, try to focus on the content of your presentation via an old-fashioned outline and then practice your delivery. Once you have something to say and are saying it well, then you can create some visuals that are appropriate and enhance your presentation. **PowerPoint should not come first.**

Key Take Aways

- Set key milestones for your content development.
- Be sure to allow roughly equal time for preparing and practicing your presentation. When practicing, be sure to speak it out loud.
- Plan for contingencies and be prepared if they occur.
- Slide creation comes at the end of your presentation development process. Define your speaking goal based on your audience and their needs in relationship to your topic. Then, and only then, consider if slides will help your audience understand your point.

AcTivity

Come up with three possible challenges you might have in delivering an upcoming presentation, such as your slides don't project. Develop a contingency plan for each (e.g., have print outs ready to hand out).

Challenge:

_____

_____

_____

Contingency:

_____

_____

_____

Challenge:

_____

_____

_____

Contingency:

_____

_____

_____

Challenge:

_____

_____

_____

Contingency:

_____

_____

_____

CHAPTER 6
Putting It All Together

PUTTING IT ALL TOGETHER

Finding the right anxiety management technique or blend of techniques that will work for you is more art than science. Ideally, you want to find the techniques that fit best with your personality, experience, and needs. As you encountered each of the techniques described in this book, you likely felt that some would be more helpful to you than others. Take this as your starting point. Further, you might find it useful to apply some criteria to help in your technique selection. For example, do you prefer to start with anxiety management techniques that are tied to content (e.g., focusing your practice via chunking, practicing commencing)? Or would you like to focus on techniques that can be employed immediately before speaking (e.g., belly breathing, tongue twisters)? Finally, would you prefer to make use of more generic anxiety management techniques (e.g., mindfulness, positive affirmations)?

Once you have a list of specific techniques, begin to incorporate them into your speech preparation and life. Many of these techniques require practice and patience, but with perseverance they should help you feel calmer and more confident. Don't be afraid to eliminate one or two techniques if they don't work for you. Experiment by combining techniques or changing the order in which you practice them.

Try this: Refer to Appendix E (Anxiety Management Techniques). Identify three to five techniques and suggestions that you feel would be most useful to you.

REAL-WORLD ANXIETY MANAGEMENT PLANS (AMPs)

To demonstrate how to make these techniques your own, meet Craig, Alicia, and Jayden. Craig is an executive whom I have coached. His fear of speaking in front of audiences is deeply rooted, and it is the one part of his job that he used to dread. Craig had been told that he often comes off as nervous because he fails to connect with his audience. Based on his introspection and my interrogation, Craig concluded that his speaking anxiety is goal based. Because of his organizational role, he is repeatedly in a position to ask partners and prospects to do things they likely do not want to do. He used to come to these presentations feeling there was one right way to deliver so that he could achieve his goal and get what he wanted from his audience members.

After reviewing the same techniques that you just read about, Craig and I identified four that not only felt good and reasonable to him, but also helped him address the underlying issues of his anxiety. First, Craig prepares and practices presentations as if he is having a <u>conversation</u>. He routinely sits with a few of his direct reports over coffee and practices his presentations. Second, before speaking, Craig is sure to focus on the positive <u>affirmation</u> we created. Before starting, he says, "I enjoy connecting with each member of my audience." Third, Craig <u>looks confident</u> by using the "fake it until you make it" eye contact trick of looking at the spaces between his audience members' eyebrows. Fourth, when he begins to feel anxious, Craig relies on the <u>mindfulness</u> technique of distancing himself from his anxious feelings by saying, "This is me feeling nervous." We dubbed his anxiety management plan *C.A.L.M.* This mnemonic helps Craig remember the four techniques and has the added benefit of reminding him of his goal.

Craig's C.A.L.M. anxiety management techniques

- ▶ **C**onverse with the audience.
- ▶ **A**ffirm abilities.
- ▶ **L**ook confident.
- ▶ **M**indful focus.

Like Craig, Alicia uses a memory aid to remind her of her anxiety management plan. Her mnemonic is *B.R.A.V.E.* Alicia was born in Europe and learned English in adolescence. While at university, she had to deliver a speech in class. She felt the presentation had

gone poorly, and to add insult to injury, her professor
told her she was the worst presenter in class. Since that
day several decades ago, Alicia has experienced extreme
situation-based speaking anxiety. As part of a require-
ment for her new career aspirations, Alicia took one of
my public speaking classes. Together, Alicia and I identified her *B.R.A.V.E.* anxiety management plan. First,
Alicia finds that her anxiety is lessened when she can
<u>be present oriented</u>. To aid in focusing on the present,
she relies on her avid enjoyment of Sudoku. Just before
speaking, she will complete a Sudoku puzzle. Second,
Alicia walks through a <u>rationalization</u> process when her
fear flares up. She writes out her fears and reassures her-
self that her biggest fear is unlikely to be realized. Third,
to connect to her audience, Alicia makes her approach
to authoring her presentation <u>audience centric</u> by starting from the fundamental question "What does my
audience need to hear from me?" Fourth, she practices
a <u>visualization</u> of her impending speech twice a day
beginning three days before presenting. Fifth, Alicia
finds that <u>exercising</u> regularly gives her perspective on
her fear and helps her to sleep better at night.

<u>Alicia's B.R.A.V.E. anxiety management techniques</u>

▶ **B**e present oriented.
▶ **R**ationally confront your speaking fear.
▶ **A**ddress what your audience needs to know.
▶ **V**isualize a successful presentation experience.
▶ **E**xercise.

Unlike Craig and Alicia, Jayden came up with a speaking anxiety management plan that did not require developing new skills. Rather, he needed to stop enacting behaviors that made his anxiety worse. Jayden is an assistant professor who can effortlessly lecture to his students, but he experiences severe anxiety when he must address his peers. His speaking anxiety is specific to the audience to whom he presents. Upon analysis, we discovered that Jayden's tendency to procrastinate worsens his anxiety. Typically, Jayden would wait until the last minute to start creating his PowerPoint slides. He could easily have started earlier, but he continually found himself staying up all night prior to his presentation feverishly authoring slides while downing multiple caffeine-filled Red Bulls. By the time he was ready to present, Jayden was jittery, unfocused, and rushed. He would end up reading his wordy slides and not engaging his audience. Together, Jayden and I developed a new presentation writing process for him. To begin, Jayden starts writing his presentation outline-not his PowerPoint slides-a week in advance of his delivery date. Once he has a detailed outline complete, then he begins creating his slides. With his outline done and a few slides created, Jayden begins to practice his presentation at least two days prior to the delivery date. This process is well documented in a formal schedule that he shares with his wife. In fact, they place the schedule on their refrigerator. This public posting helps keep Jayden focused. Jayden makes sure to work on his presentation after he eats a healthy lunch devoid of caffeine. It was not easy for Jayden to cease his bad habits. Now that he has separated presentation writing from PowerPoint slide creation, altered his diet, and publicly committed to his speech development and practice plan, he finds himself less stressed and is delivering better presentations to his colleagues.

Craig, Alicia, and Jayden have made great strides toward managing their speaking fears. They feel empowered over their anxiety and credit this shift to their dedicated work and their use of their anxiety management plans. I encourage you to find one or more techniques that can lead you to the kind of success Craig, Alicia, and Jayden enjoy.

Try **Try this:** Create your own anxiety management plan, complete with an acronym to help you remember it.

CONCLUSION

Communication apprehension can be debilitating. The fear associated with speaking or anticipating giving a presentation can lead to many negative outcomes. Learning techniques to minimize this anxiety can help you become a more confident and competent communicator.

You now have a deeper understanding of speaking anxiety and 50 techniques to help you manage it. As with any learning, you will need to dedicate time to practicing them. Not all of these techniques will work for you. Think about the ones that you connect with, and try them out. Avoid panicking if you don't notice immediate improvement. These techniques take time to refine before they can become part of your repertoire. Regardless of the techniques you choose, simply knowing that you can have a dramatic impact on your speaking anxiety is empowering.

Remember, the focus of your presentation needs to be on your audience–not you. You need to get out of your own way, so that you can feel confident, calm, and competent in speaking up without freaking out!

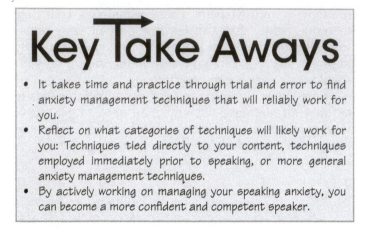

Key Take Aways

- It takes time and practice through trial and error to find anxiety management techniques that will reliably work for you.
- Reflect on what categories of techniques will likely work for you: Techniques tied directly to your content, techniques employed immediately prior to speaking, or more general anxiety management techniques.
- By actively working on managing your speaking anxiety, you can become a more confident and competent speaker.

AcTivity

Create your own Anxiety Management Plan (AMP). Come up with a meaningful acronym, such as those found in Chapter 6 of the text, to help you remember your AMP. Identify each technique and detail how/when you will use each technique.

_____

_____

_____

_____

_____

_____

_____

_____

_____

_____

_____

_____

_____

Appendix A: The Audience Beyond the Room

Audiences now extend far beyond the confines of the room in which a speaker presents. Your words can potentially be heard all over the globe for a long time after you have spoken them. Conference calls, tweets, YouTube videos, WebEx meetings, and the like multiply the size and range of your audience—and possibly your nervousness. Two major anxieties tend to develop as a result of the audience beyond the room. First, you might experience "fear of the faceless." Looking out into your audience's eyes can be daunting, for sure, but it can be even more worrisome *not* to see your audience at all: Is my audience on the other end of the conference call interested? Does my audience participating in my web presentation agree with me? Is the audience watching my online video presentation snickering at my ideas? The fear of these unknowns can be quite distracting. Second, you might experience "concern over the integrity of your content." Technology makes it very easy to have your words truncated, taken out of context, or misrepresented. Audience members' tweets and blogs provide great conduits to extend the reach of your message, but those doing the tweeting and blogging might also alter your message and its meaning. Anxiety levels can rise when you worry about losing control of your content.

Short of traveling back in time or completely disconnecting from the modern technological world, you need to accept that at times you will not see all of your audience members nor have complete control over your message. This acceptance can help reduce your anxiety by allowing you to focus on what you do have influence over. In addition, you can employ a few anxiety reduction techniques to manage fears that result from the audience beyond the room.

Anxiety arising from not seeing your audience can be addressed by giving a face to the faceless. When presenting via conference call or the web, **envision people who you know listening to your presentation**. Imagining supportive people who you know receiving your message helps assuage your fear because your message has friendly ears on which to land, and you are likely to be more engaged since you are speaking to known audience members. As a potentially helpful aside, research from the 1980s suggests that envisioning beloved pets can also reduce anxiety.

Try **Try this:** In advance of presenting in a mediated fashion (e.g., via web presentation or conference call), write a list of supportive people you can imagine having in your audience. When your presentation occurs, act as if you are presenting to these people.

One way to manage anxiety arising from concerns over your content being manipulated after you present is to **make your messages concise and repetitive**. Research suggests that succinct messages are more memorable and likely to maintain their fidelity, which means that there is less likelihood of your message being altered. Useful techniques you can try include: (1) stripping away excess wording that might sound good when read silently but adds limited value when spoken, and (2) prior to presenting, asking others to paraphrase your points to see if their wording is more succinct. Additionally, you can use creative repetition to reinforce your message, which again reduces the chances of the message being changed or diluted. Creative repetition includes providing examples, facts, analogies, or stories that demonstrate your point or show what you are trying to convey.

Try **Try this:** When constructing your content, ask yourself continually how your message could be more concise. Challenge yourself to get your point across as simply and succinctly as possible. Further, find one or two stories, examples, statistics, and the like that restate your point.

With a little extra time and some creative imagination, you can reduce anxiety that originate from the audience beyond the room.

Appendix B: Anxiety Management for Non-native English Speakers

---

Having to speak in public can produce enough anxiety, but if you are not a native speaker, you might find that speaking in front of others is a truly frightening experience. The anxiety management techniques presented in this book are equally valuable to non-native speakers. However, two other suggestions might help relieve the added anxiety brought on by speaking in a different language. First, it helps to understand the audience's expectations of native English speakers. Second, if you are concerned about having a heavy accent, there are a few things that you can do.

As pointed out in the discussion of the "fake it until you make it" approach in Chapter 1, audience members expect nervous speakers to do certain things. They also expect good communicators to do certain things. These expectations are different in different cultures. For example, competent English speakers from the United States (and Canada) make eye contact, they gesture frequently, and they move around the room. A person who is relatively new to the language, and perhaps to culture, needs to understand what the audience is expecting from his or her delivery. In other words, you must try to **determine the cultural expectations of your audience**. To do this, you can (1) ask trusted peers, (2) observe competent speakers, and/or (3) try out what you think is appropriate and see how people respond. Regardless of how you determine the expectations that your audience might have, you need to conform to these expectations.

Try

Try this: List five to seven of the expectations that your audience will have for a competent speaker. Next, develop a plan to practice these skills in your delivery. Consider capturing your practice on video to see if you are conforming to these expectations.

Many non-native speakers have accents. The added worry about whether the audience will be able to understand what is being said weighs heavily on non-native speakers. This added anxiety often leads speakers who have accents to speak very quickly. This almost ensures that the audience will not understand them.

Practicing your pronunciation and finding a program for accent reduction are two options, but an easier technique exists. Audience members are more likely to accept an accented speaker if the speaker simply begins his or her presentation more slowly. Choose an introductory sentence or two that are not vitally important to your presentation and **speak more slowly than you usually do**. This slower speech rate allows your audience to adapt and adjust to your accent.

Try this: Craft one or two sentences to begin your talk that acknowledge your audience and/or speaking situation (e.g., "I am honored to be here to discuss my topic with you."). Practice delivering your opening line(s) at a slower rate than usual. It might be helpful to you to audio or video record these first sentences so that you can hear if you are speaking more slowly.

Being a non-native speaker adds some extra hurdles to managing your speaking anxiety, but with dedicated practice and extra attention, you can reap the rewards of lessened nervousness.

Appendix C: Reducing Disfluencies: Cleaning Up Verbal Graffiti

My clients and students often ask me: "How can a presenter reduce the number of "uh's" and "um's"? These disfluencies, sometimes referred to as "verbal graffiti" or "vocal tics," appear to be universal–academics have found that people in every culture have them and that they can make up to 20 percent of what is spoken in everyday conversation. What people say when they fill their pauses vary, though. North Americans tend to say "um" and "uh," while those from Asia are more likely to say "ah" and "oh."

Regardless of what you say or where you are in the world, you don't plan to use disfluencies when presenting. They are the unconscious byproduct of thinking while speaking, and they happen much more frequently if that thinking occurs when you are speaking in more formal presentation situations. While "um's" and "uh's" occur in casual conversation, they are far more frequent when public speaking. Unlike conversation, where we share the speaking duties with others, the pressure of having everyone listening to us seems to invite us to fill our thinking pauses.

However, not all disfluencies are experienced in the same way by your audience. "Um's" and "uh's" within sentences are not perceived as frequently, nor are they as bothersome as those that occur between thoughts. Your audience often skips over mid-sentence disfluencies because they are more focused on your content than your verbal delivery. Yet, as you move from one point to the other, disfluencies stand out because your audience is no longer "distracted" by what you are saying. In essence, you are violating your audience's expectation of a silent pause by filling the silence.

Verbal graffiti littering your presentations leads your audience at a minimum to perceive you as nervous. However, many disfluencies also lead to perceptions of deceit or being unprepared. Additionally, disfluencies can be very distracting for your audience. They begin to count your disfluencies, rather than focus on what counts—namely your content. So, you need to reduce disfluencies to be seen as a more confident, credible communicator and to help your audience focus on your message.

The following two techniques will assist you in eliminating disfluencies:

First, gain conscious control over using disfluencies. To do this, you need someone to notify you every time you say "um" or "uh" while presenting. This notification can come in the form of a raised hand, a clap, or in my case, a request for service bell like those found in hotels. By notifying you of your disfluencies immediately after you speak them, you begin to become consciously aware of your saying them. Once aware, and over time, you can begin to reduce the frequency of your disfluencies because they are more under your control.

Try **Try this:** When practicing a portion of your presentation, have a friend raise his or her hand to **notify you when you speak a disfluency**. Rather than stopping your speaking, continue your presentation and just make a mental note that the disfluency occurred.

Second, when ending your sentences, especially your major points, do so on an exhale. By doing this, you must necessarily start your next thought with an inhalation. It is impossible to say "um" while inhaling. In addition to eliminating between thought disfluencies, your inhalation brings a pause with it. This unfilled pause has the added benefit of giving your audience a break to process your ideas, while fulfilling their expectation that you will briefly stop speaking prior to moving on.

Try **Try this: Practice exhaling completely** at the end of your spoken sentences by reciting a list of sentences (e.g., walk through the steps of a recipe or your favorite things to do on a weekend). As you end each sentence, be sure to exhale completely. For example:

- I enjoy making peanut butter sandwiches (exhale completely).

- First, I toast the bread (exhale completely).

- Next, I spread the peanut butter evenly on both sides of the toast (exhale completely).
- Finally, after combining the halves, I enjoy the sandwich with a cold drink (exhale completely).

As a speaker, you want your audience to be compelled by your message and not distracted by your delivery. You want them to see you as confident, not nervous or deceitful. By addressing disfluencies, you achieve both of these goals.

Appendix D: Commanding the Room with Confidence During Q&A

Mustering the courage to present confidently in front of others is hard enough, but when it comes to actually engaging an audience and managing their participation during a question and answer (Q&A) session, many presenters freak out. Making this switch from monologue to dialogue is a challenge for both the audience and speaker alike, but it's necessary if you want to allow for questions. Your audience needs you to lead them through this transition. They expect you to confidently "command the room" and help them to participate.

The quick switch to interactivity and a more equal balance of status and power can be confusing and challenging to you and your audience. However, there are simple actions you can take to help you navigate smoothly and calmly into and through your Q&A session.

Prior to presenting, you should spend time reflecting on the questions you might receive on your topic. You might need to do some reconnaissance to figure out your potential questions, such as asking people similar to those that will be in your audience, querying FAQ lists or customer/prospect databases, etc. Once you have some potential questions, you can begin to think about how you might answer them. As mentioned in Chapter 5, thinking about what you intend to say is not enough. You also need to practice standing and delivering your answers. Simply knowing what you might encounter during the Q&A session can help reduce your anxiety.

Try **Try this:** After you have structured your presentation's content, **reflect on possible questions you might be asked**. Decide if you should alter your content to address these questions in the body of your presentation, or start to generate answers to the questions and actually practice delivering these answers.

To begin, you need to consider when to take questions from your audience. My advice is to take your questions at the end of your presentation if you are a nervous speaker. This compartmentalization allows you to stay focused on the task at hand—presenting or answering questions. If you are a more seasoned speaker or have content that is very complex, you should consider taking questions throughout your presentation at designated times that you define for your audience at the beginning of your presentation.

When it comes time to ask your audience for their questions, you need to solicit their queries in a way that maintains your credibility and authority while being humble, open, and responsive. This transition to an actual conversation with your audience can be tricky, but it can be made easier by (1) the expectations you establish when you call for questions, and (2) how you actually collect the questions that you intend to answer.

Too often, Q&A sessions are opened with generic invitations like "Are there any questions?" Broad invitations such as this are often too open ended for audience members to come up with focused, concrete questions. Rather, I suggest asking for the exact type of questions that you desire to answer. For example, "I would like to spend 5–10 minutes answering questions about the solution that I provided." This more restrictive opening helps your audience know what types of questions to ask, establishes you as being in control, and leads to questions that you are prepared to answer.

It is important to reflect on the anxiety involved in the Q&A session. As the presenter, it is easy to understand anxiety that you might feel, but audience members also experience nervousness during the Q&A session. While you have had a chance to warm up and become comfortable with speaking in your environment, audience members do not have this advantage. Further, they are feeling the influence of several pressures. First, audience members might fear looking stupid and foolish by asking a question. Second, they may be highly sensitive to the power dynamics (e.g., the boss being present) or societal norms (e.g., it is disrespectful to question a speaker). Finally, audience members might not want to put you on the spot and make you look bad. Unfortunately, as a presenter who desires good, interactive questions, you must take on the added burden of helping your audience get their questions to you. To assist your audience in asking questions, allow for time after your initial call for their inquiries. It takes a little time for them to formulate questions as well as to muster up the courage to ask them. If you do not get an initial question, have one ready to ask yourself. For example, you can say: "I am often asked:."

When accumulating questions, you have a few options available that go beyond the standard call and respond methodology. The first is to prioritize the questions coming in. In an online presentation platform, you should be able to flag questions that come in as your presenting so when you get to the Q&A, you already have some questions to start answering. As new questions come in, it may help to have someone online with you to filter and ask the questions to you so you can stay focused on your answers. When presenting in front of a live audience, you can request that audience members write down their questions on notecards (or post them via text messages). This allows for some degree of anonymity for the asker and allows you to prioritize which questions you would like to answer. Next, you can follow the lead of famous venture capitalist John Doeer and solicit all questions first—writing them down—and then answer them in the order you wish. Like the written approach above, you can prioritize and link questions together.

When answering questions, paraphrase the question asked. This confers several benefits to you: (1) you validate and reward the asker, which will likely encourage more participation—although avoid saying "good question" to every query, (2) it ensures you will answer the correct question(s), (3) if you can paraphrase and also think of an answer at the same time, you buy yourself a little preparation time, and (4) you can reframe an emotional or challenging question to be better suited for you; for example, a question such as "Your pricing is ridiculously expensive: How do you get away with charging so much?" can be rephrased as "You are asking about our product's value."

Nonverbally, Q&A online should be done with video conferencing if possible. This visual connection not only allows your nonverbal communication to engage your audience, but it also lessens your nervousness. When responding, remember to address your answer to the entire audience and deliver your answers in the same speaking style—cadence, vocal variation, etc.—as you used during your presentation. You want to avoid becoming a different speaker in terms of your delivery. One powerful nonverbal action you can take to demonstrate your confidence is to step forward toward the question asker while listening to the query.

To help your audience understand your answers, **invoke the A.D.D. method of answering questions**:

- **A**nswer the question (one clear, declarative sentence).

- **D**etail a specific, concrete example that supports your answer.
- **D**escribe the benefits that explain why your answer is relevant to the asker.

An example A.D.D. answer to the question, "Describe your qualifications for a job as a communication coach."

- **A**nswer = "I have over 20 years of experience helping people improve their communication skills."
- **D**etail = "I have helped line employees and executives learn to be more confident and compelling presenters. Just last week, I worked with an executive at a large, local firm on a major keynote she had."
- **D**escribe = "What this means for you is that my experience will allow me to immediately help you with your specific needs."

Try **Try this:** After generating a list of possible questions, practice answering the questions using the A.D.D. (**A**nswer > provide **D**etail > **D**escribe the value to the asker). Take the time not only to generate the content of your answer, but practice speaking the answer as well.

The final step in a confidently managed Q&A session is to return to your core message prior to ending your talk. Too often nervous speakers end Q&A with a quick "thank you" and an even quicker exit from the stage. You want to end with impact, so be sure to thank your audience and concisely restate your central message. This ensures that the last thing your audience hears is what you want them to leave with.

Taken all together, your pre-work and preparation for managing a Q&A session can dramatically reduce your nervousness over this anxiety-provoking spontaneous speaking situation.

Appendix E: Anxiety Management Techniques

Anxiety Management Technique	What to Do
Relabel and greet anxious arousal	When you experience negative physical arousal (e.g., your heart rate increases, you begin to sweat), remind yourself that these reactions are normal and typical. They are your body's normal response to something that is displeasing. Avoid giving them greater negative significance. Greet these natural responses by saying to yourself: "Here are those anxiety feelings again. Of course, I should be feeling them, I am about to give a presentation."

(*continued*)

Anxiety Management Technique	What to Do
Fake it until you make it	Catalog behaviors of competent and confident speakers. Note their use of eye contact and their stance, movement, and gestures. Mimic some of these actions. Soon you will begin to feel more confident and competent.
Audio record yourself and practice while listening	Audio record yourself delivering your presentation, then play the recording back while you stand and practice your gestures. Since you do not have to think about what to say, practicing in this manner allows you to focus on your gestures and other nonverbal behaviors.
Reduce your core body temperature	Hold something cold in the palms of your hands—a chilled bottle of water is ideal. The cold will reduce your body temperature and reduce the sweating and flushing that result from increased blood flow.
Give your nervous energy a place to go	Secretly squeeze your toes or lightly squeeze your thumb and pointer finger together in your non-gesturing hand. These activities allow you to rid yourself of this excess energy and eliminate your shakiness.

(*continued*)

Anxiety Management Technique	What to Do
Acknowledge the benefits of managed speaking anxiety	Remind yourself that managed speaking anxiety helps you to focus and to see things clearly, provides you with energy, motivates you to care about your communicative outcomes, and encourages you to prepare. Further, it helps your audience to feel comfortable and, thus, focus on your message.
Develop needed skills	Take steps to develop your presentation skills. Read books; watch and analyze video clips of effective speakers.
Collaborate with others	Attend public speaking classes, join speaking organizations (e.g., Toastmasters), or find others wishing to improve.
Participate in an improvisation class	Join an improvisation class or workshop. Through collaboration and a safe environment, improvisation activities teach speakers to be calm under pressure and that being in front of others can be fun.

(*continued*)

Anxiety Management Technique	What to Do
Breathe slowly and deeply	Take a slow, deep inhalation through your nose and fill your lower abdomen. Slowly release your breath through your nose. To occupy your mind, slowly count to three as you inhale and then again as you exhale. Focus your attention on the counting. Repeat several times.
Dress appropriately and comfortably	Take time to determine an appropriate wardrobe for your presentation. Consider the expectations of your speaking situation and audience. You want to be comfortable in your appearance and avoid any distractions that your clothing or accessories might provide. Be sure to practice delivering your talk in your presentation clothes and shoes.
Practice commencing	Write out and practice your first sentences. These can express gratitude to your audience or acknowledge the person introducing you, the speaking venue, or the opportunity you've been given to speak. While commencing your talk, scan the room so that you can get a handle on your speaking environment.

(continued)

Anxiety Management Technique	What to Do
Visualize	Walk yourself through an ideal speaking experience. Focus holistically on your entire speaking day, culminating in a successful presentation. Try to get yourself relaxed and see positive things happening throughout the day. Avoid getting into the details of what you say. Be sure to begin your visualizations several days before your actual presentation.
Document your successes at presenting	Delineate your presenting successes and identify the factors that contributed to your success. What did you do, what didn't you do, and was there something about the audience or context that brought about your success? Once you have identified these factors, you can replicate them in your future preparation, practice, and performance.
Precipitate oxytocin flooding	Shake hands with or hug audience members prior to speaking. This physical connection stimulates the release of the neurotransmitter oxytocin, which will produce a calming effect.

(*continued*)

Anxiety Management Technique	What to Do
Act courageously prior to speaking	Volunteer to present first, ask a question of the previous speaker, or introduce the speaker who presents before you. These brave acts release neurotransmitters that will reduce your nervous symptoms caused by cortisol and adrenaline.
Use systematic desensitization	Identify five increasingly threatening steps in delivering a speech. Begin by relaxing yourself, and think about the least threatening of the steps you just identified. At the first sign of anxiety, being your relaxation practice. Repeat this process until you can envision the threat without having your trigger fire. You are now ready to begin again with the next threatening step you identified.
Use sequential muscle relaxation	Tense and relax your toes while breathing slowly and deeply. Work your way up your entire body until you tense and relax your forehead. When done, you should feel more relaxed and with fuller, calmer breathing.

(*continued*)

Anxiety Management Technique	What to Do
Reframe the speaking situation as a conversation	Invite a friend or two to sit with you, and talk over with them your presentation. You are not presenting or performing, but rather conversing. No longer will you feel the pressure of there being only one right way to present.
Create and use positive affirmations	Create a short, memorable, and reasonable positive affirmation. Rehearse it aloud. You will be empowered by hearing the affirmation. Make your affirmation the last thing you say to yourself before you begin to speak.
Be optimistic about future activities	Generate a list of things that you can look forward to after you present. These can be activities or items. By imagining optimistic outcomes unrelated to and beyond your presentation, you will be less anxious during the presentation.
Practice mindfulness	Say, "This is me feeling anxiety," when you next feel nervous about speaking. Experience the space this affords you. Notice that you can think about and evaluate your feelings more clearly.

(continued)

Anxiety Management Technique	What to Do
Rationally confront your speaking fear	Identify your biggest fear about presenting. Next, think about the worst thing that could happen to you and your audience if the specific fear came true. Finally, select a likelihood percentage of this fear coming true for you in your next speech. Notice that your fears are not imminent or highly likely. If they were to come true, the result would not be devastating.
Write down your fears	Put your fears on paper. This offloads them and makes your fears become less personal (they become "the" fears, not "your" fears). The words you use to describe the experience of your fears influences the effect writing about them has. When writing about your anxiety over a past presentation and its effects on you, use the past tense. For example, "I forgot my second point" versus "I keep forgetting my points."
Verbally state how your fear is making you feel	Verbalize your fears explicitly in writing or speaking. Use negative words to describe how you are feeling; this increases the anxiety reduction. For example, "I am *terrified* of that *scary* speaking situation where I am *likely to forget* my points and *embarrass* myself in front of my colleagues."

(continued)

Anxiety Management Technique	What to Do
Maintain a present-oriented focus	Use techniques that create an expanded present moment where you do not think about future consequences. Listen to music, do physical activity, say a tongue twister, play a video game.
Focus on your audience	Ask yourself, "What does my audience need to know about the topic?" and "How can I ensure that they get the information they need?" The answers to these two questions move you away from thinking that there is only one right way to speak.
Make sure your points are relevant	Focus on the key take away(s) for your audience. At the end of each major point you make, think to yourself how you would end the sentence: "The bottom line for you is:." While you might not actually speak these lines at the end of each of your points, you will be sure to focus on each point's relevance to your audience, which in turn, will make you more confident because you will know that they are getting what then need from your presentation.

(*continued*)

Anxiety Management Technique	What to Do
ACTs invite audience participation and reduce your nervousness	Audience-connecting techniques (ACTs) engage your audience, which helps you feel less nervous because your audience is actively working with you. Try asking a polling question, have your audience imagine something, use a think-pair-share activity, or step toward your audience when you speak.
Use a strong introduction to your presentation	Introductions help your audience feel more connected and comfortable, which in turn, makes you feel more comfortable. Start by getting your audience's attention and then explain why they should listen to your talk. Finally, let them know what is coming next by previewing your upcoming points
Create and stick to a meal plan	Create a meal plan or menu that itemizes the food and drink you will consume before writing, preparing, and presenting your speech. Foods containing complex carbohydrates and monounsaturated fats are good to eat. Have these foods handy so that you won't be tempted to indulge in less wise choices.

(*continued*)

Anxiety Management Technique	What to Do
Create and stick to an exercise plan	Design an exercise plan that gets you outdoors (e.g., walking, swimming, hiking). Prior to working on your presentation, take 20 minutes to enact your exercise plan. Note how much calmer you are, and observe how much sharper you feel mentally after you are done exercising.
Manage your sleep schedule	Go to bed and wake up at your regular times. Avoid altering your sleep-wake schedule. If you find yourself ruminating over your presentation while trying to fall asleep, keep a notebook by your pillow so that you can write down your thoughts and release their hold on you.
Take time to play	Consciously make time to play with your pet, children, or friends. Even short bursts of play can sharpen your mind and improve your spirits.
Practice state-dependent learning	Reflect on the characteristics of the room in which you will be presenting. Better yet, go explore it if you can. When you prepare and practice your presentation, try to do so in a room similar in design, noise level, brightness, and the like.

(*continued*)

Anxiety Management Technique	What to Do
Create a content learning plan	Create a content learning plan that includes blocks of study time, varied parts of your presentation to learn, and specific questions that you can use to test how well you are remembering your content.
Provide a meaningful structure to your content	Place your content in a structure to help you and your audience better remember your content. Useful structures include problem-solution-benefit as well as what?-so what?-now what?
Create a public schedule	Create a public schedule for the development and practicing of your presentation. Identify three incentives that motivate you. Use these incentives as rewards for accomplishing the itemized presentation milestones you have chosen.
Engage in focused practice	Chunk your presentation into logical units, such as introduction, conclusion, point 1, transitions, and the like. Practice each part until you feel comfortable and more relaxed with each chunk.
Develop contingency plans	Identify three to five things that could cause you problems when you present. With these potential problems in mind, develop an action plan for each one.

(*continued*)

Anxiety Management Technique	What to Do
Present in a well-lit room	Being in a dark environment increases anxiety. Try to have lights up and on when presenting.
Use PowerPoint wisely	Author your content in an outline format before you create slides. Next, determine if and what slides are needed. Then, create slides. This process reduces the time spent on slide creation and allows for more time to be spent practicing.
Envision people who you know listening to your presentation	Write a list of supportive people who you can imagine having in your audience. When your presentation occurs, act as if you are presenting to these people.
Make your messages concise and repetitive	Strip away excess wording and ask others to paraphrase your points to see if their wording is more succinct. Use creative repetition to reinforce your message (e.g., examples, stories, statistics).
Determine the cultural expectations of your audience	List five to seven of the expectations that your audience will have for a competent speaker. Next, develop a plan to practice these skills in your delivery.

(*continued*)

Anxiety Management Technique	What to Do
Begin your presentation speaking slightly more slowly	Craft one or two sentences to begin your talk that acknowledge your audience and/or speaking situation. Practice delivering your opening line(s) at a slower rate than usual.
Get notified every time you speak a disfluency	Have someone alert you when you speak a disfluency. This notification can come in the form of a raised hand or a clap. By notifying you of your disfluencies immediately after you speak them, you begin to become consciously aware of your saying them. Once aware, and over time, you can begin to reduce the frequency of your disfluencies because they are more under your control.
End your sentences with a complete exhalation	Completely exhale at the end of your sentences, especially your major points. This means you will start your next thought with an inhalation. It is impossible to say "um" while inhaling.
Reflect on possible questions that you might be asked	Think about what questions might come up during your Q&A session. This preparation reduces the anxiety you may have over the unexpected, challenging questions that could arise.

(continued)

Anxiety Management Technique	What to Do
Use A.D.D. to answer questions	After generating a list of possible questions, practice answering the questions using the A.D.D. (Answer > provide Detail > Describe the value to the asker). Take the time not only to generate the content of your answer, but practice speaking the answer as well.

Glossary

Anxiety sensitivity A person's degree of responsiveness to threatening (i.e., fear-inducing) stimuli.

Attribution Explanation ascribed to a particular behavior. It can be positive or negative.

Choking An anxiety response that leads to too much thinking. A speaker's thoughts become jumbled and he or she becomes overly self-conscious.

Cognitive demand (cognitive load) The requirements that a particular task, such as worrying about a speech, place on a person's ability to think and process information.

Cognitive modification Similar to reappraisal (see definition below).

Commencing The interval between pre-speaking silence and the beginning utterances of a presentation.

Communication apprehension Fear associated with either real or anticipated speaking.

Conditioning The learned pairing or association of two unrelated stimuli (e.g., public speaking is nerve-wracking).

Descriptive gestures Gestures that demonstrate or show what you are verbally describing.

Disfluencies Verbal interruptions in the normal flow of speech, such as repeating of words, stuttering, or using filler words (e.g., "um," "uh," and "ah").

Emphatic gestures Gestures that provide emphasis to what you are verbally saying.

Extemporaneous speaking Presenting that is prepared but not memorized. Often, this type of speaking is highly engaging and conversational in tone.

Extinguish To replace or remove a conditioned association.

Fear response The automatic physiological arousal triggered by a threat, such as public speaking. Also known as the fight, flight, fright, or freeze response.

Habituation Reduction in speaking anxiety that follows the first minute of speaking. Attributed to the comfort that comes with making it through the first part of a presentation without major problems.

Implementation intention Establishing specific actions that are tied to desired goals that help short-circuit procrastination (e.g., setting an alarm clock the night before prevents oversleeping so that you can make an early morning appointment).

Interoceptive sensitivity The sensitivity to stimuli coming from within the body (e.g., feeling the increase in heart rate associated with anxiety).

Leakage The unwanted revealing of one's emotional state via nonverbal cues.

Overlearning The learning that occurs when a particular skill is repeated or practiced so frequently that the skill becomes automated and, thus, requires less mental effort to perform.

Panicking An anxiety response that leads to a lack of clear thinking and an inability to maintain focus.

Reappraisal (reframing) Cognitive switching in the interpretation of a situation or stimulus from one perspective (e.g., presenting as performance) to another (e.g., presenting as a conversation).

Relaxation-induced anxiety The extra nervousness some people feel when they try hard to relax after their fear response has been activated.

Self-fulfilling prophecy A process by which the expectation that a result will happen leads to the occurrence of that result through conscious or unconscious effort in support of the goal.

Solutions-focused therapy A type of talk therapy where patient and therapist focus on events, regardless of how small or brief, where the patient has had some success in achieving his or her desired goal or behavior. These successes are explored in an attempt to learn from them.

State-based communication apprehension Anxiety brought on by factors external to the speaker, such as context, audience, or goal.

State-dependent learning The notion that you remember more information more accurately if you recall the information in an environment similar to the environment in which you learned the information.

Trait-based communication anxiety Innate anxiety resulting from genetic predispositions. Synonyms for this type of anxiety are shyness and introversion.

Visualization The process of forming a mental imagine of your actions or performance. This technique is very effective in improving performance and managing performance anxiety.

Bibliography

Ayers, J., and Hopf, T. (1993). *Coping with Speech Anxiety.*
New York: Ablex Publishing.

Beilock, S. (2010). *Choke: What Secrets of the Brain Reveal about Getting It Right When You Have To.* New York: Simon & Schuster Publishing.

Bodie, G. D. (2010). A Racing Heart, Rattling Knees, and Ruminative Thoughts: Defining, Explaining, and Treating Public Speaking Anxiety. *Communication Education, 59,* 70—105.

Clark, T. (2011). *Nerve: Poise Under Pressure, Serenity Under Stress, and the Brave New Science of Fear and Cool.* New York: Little, Brown and Company.

Csikszentmihalyi, M. (2008). *Flow: The Psychology of Optimal Experience.* New York: Harper Perennial Modern Classics.

Daly, J. A., and McCroskey, J. C. (1984). *Avoiding Communication: Shyness, Reticence, and Communication Apprehension.* Newbury Park, CA: Sage.

Lyubomirsky, S. (2007). *The How of Happiness: A New Approach to Getting the Life You Want.* New York: Penguin Books.

Motley, M. T. (1997). *Overcoming Your Fear of Public Speaking: A Proven Method.* Boston: Houghton Mifflin.

Richmond, V. P., and McCroskey, J. C. (1998). *Communication Apprehension, Avoidance, and Effectiveness*, 5th ed. Boston: Allyn and Bacon.

Tolle, Eckhart. (2004). *The Power of Now: A Guide to Spiritual Enlightenment.* Novato, CA: New World Library.

Wehrenberg, M., and Prinz, S. (2007). *The Anxious Brain: The Neurobiological Basis of Anxiety Disorders and How to Effectively Treat Them.* New York: Norton.

Wise, J. (2009). *Extreme Fear: The Science of Your Mind in Danger.* New York: Macmillan.

About the Author

Matt Abrahams is a passionate, collaborative, and innovative teacher who teaches strategic communication at Stanford University's Graduate School of Business as well as public speaking, group communication, and improvisation at Stanford University's Continuing Studies Program and De Anza College. He is especially interested in applying communication knowledge to real-world issues. He has published several research articles on cognitive planning, persuasion, and interpersonal communication.

Prior to teaching, Matt held senior leadership positions at several software companies, where he created and ran global training and development organizations. In addition to his teaching and research activities, Matt is co-founder of Bold Echo Communication Solutions, a successful presentation consulting and coaching practice.

Additionally, he has created two apps: eValue8 and No Freaking Speaking.

Matt received his undergraduate degree in psychology from Stanford University, his graduate degree in communication studies from the University of California at Davis, and his secondary education teaching credential from San Francisco State University.

Index